to **Wendy's**

with *Love*

the 22-year lunch

Michelle
Bleu Blessings
XOXO
Dixer

Advance Praise for *To Wendy's With Love*

"A pure delight. I smiled, giggled and cried. And through it all I felt connected. *To Wendy's With Love* has left me feeling grateful and enriched. Most of all, it inspired me to start my own 22-year lunch."
—Jen Grant, Author and Speaker, Inspiring Radiance

"Diane Keyes has captured a heartwarming story of reconciliation and connection that resonates with us all. She shares the importance of the family meal as a strong tradition in our lives that can have a ripple effect across relationships and the world. This book will make you laugh, cry, and want to re-connect with your loved ones in a deeper way. If you loved *Tuesdays with Morrie* or *The Glass Castle*, this book is your next must-read."
—Kristen Brown, Bestselling Author and Keynote Speaker

"Diane Keyes' stories are a testament to the power of connection, love, and gratitude. And in my experience, it's also a perfect example of how service industry workers can profoundly impact the lives of their customers."
—Rob Bell, Service Experience Expert, *www.RobSpeaks.com*

"*To Wendy's With Love* is a wise and powerful story of family, healing, faith and grace, and how sitting together over a meal changes lives. This book is for everyone yearning to create connection in this troubled, impersonal world. To Diane Keyes with love, thank you for writing this beautiful book."
—Barb Greenberg Founder/CEO Rediscovering U, *premier divorce support for women*

"I COULD NOT PUT THIS BOOK DOWN. *To Wendy's With Love* is the type of book that you'll wish you had written, but didn't dare. In this beautifully written memoir, Diane Keyes peels back the layers of her own life to give hope and inspiration to anyone longing for a relationship that just doesn't fit neatly into the fictional family we all idealize. The magic of this story is that it didn't take a catastrophic event to change things—all it took was saying 'yes' to lunch...and then saying yes again the next week. I highly recommend this book to *anyone* with a family. The message that sharing meals together is a way to learn to love each other again, is one that will resonate with all of us."
—Lynn Garthwaite, Author and Non-Profit Director of Books on Wings

"*To Wendy's With Love* is positively heartwarming and inspirational. It reminds me of the old Italian saying, "At the table, no one grows old." Diane Keyes invites us to pull up a chair to enjoy

and absorb the message in the meals. You will be moved to nurture and cherish your own family story."
—Jayne Morgan, Ph.D. Author of *Workplace Gems*

"As a marriage and family therapist, I often help clients find ways to foster the love and commitment needed to build and sustain relationships. Through delightful and courageous storytelling, Diane Keyes shares how her own family tradition of gathering at Wendy's for lunch, has cemented the bonds of affection and led to never-imagined good things. *To Wendy's With Love* is such inspiration, and the *perfect* blueprint for family success. I'll be recommending it often."
—Dr. Jeanne M. Wiger, Ph.D. Marriage and Family Therapist

"*To Wendy's With Love* should more aptly be titled, "*Thursdays at Wendy's*." Why? Because the author's heartwarming family story easily merits the buzz that surrounded *Tuesdays With Morrie*. Mitch Albom, watch out! Diane Keyes may be the next '*you*.'"
—Connie Anderson, Editor and Author of *When Polio Came Home*

"Absolutely incredible and touching and funny and, and, and...I sobbed, I laughed, I related. So many families have so many secrets. What would it look like if we could all have lunch once a week and repair our past? Thank you for giving me hope that

someday my own family may find their way back to each other."
—Beth M. Anderson, Sailing Captain

"*To Wendy's With Love* is a touching and humorous account of how twenty two years of weekly lunches at Wendy's fostered intergenerational healing, friendship, and joy for Diane Keyes and her extended family. Painful memories and family secrets lost their power as camaraderie and love grew with every gathering. Her story reminds us of the preciousness of a shared meal with the special people in our lives."
—Mary Treacy O'Keefe, MA, Author, Speaker, Spiritual Director

"In my decade as a TV reporter, an executive coach, and radio host, I've interviewed thousands of people. They may be newsworthy but their experiences are rarely unique. Diane Keyes' experience at Wendy's is eye-opening, authentic, and as American as a burger with fries; a story impossible to replicate. Filled with love and lessons for us all, this book is the recipe you'll wish you'd created as your own family legacy."
—Roshini Rajkumar, Presence Engineer and Host of *News & Views,* CBS Radio, Minneapolis

"Author Diane Keyes touchingly shares her experiences with family secrets and challenges in *To Wendy's With Love.* By casually

reaching out through weekly lunches, Diane and her family are able to open up, move on, and build closer relationships. Happily, this book shows us how we can bring this lesson back to our own families."
—Heidi J. Peterson, Writer and Editor

"In *To Wendy's With Love*, Diane Keyes reveals how courage, faith, and attitude can foster reconciliation anytime, anywhere. This poignant memoir illustrates that silence can wound but words can heal. Bravo, Diane."
—Caryn Sullivan, Award-winning Columnist, *Huffington Post* contributor

"A must-read, this simple, yet profoundly poignant story is a living tribute to those who choose to say 'yes' to a joy-filled life, and serves as gentle encouragement for those who have yet to find the courage. Beautifully written, *To Wendy's With Love* captures the true essence of life—the simple joy of being with individuals simply because they *are*, while its gentle message of healing speaks to the personal growth and gratitude that ascend from it."
—Patricia Johnson, Corporate Marketing Communications Director

"As a long-time member of the lunch bunch, I've witnessed many of the wonderful things that have happened over the years at Wendy's. I am happy and grateful to be included in what has become one of the highlights of my week. I'm delighted Diane has written *To Wendy's With Love* so other families can discover the secret for themselves."
—Jolene Gauss, Lunch Bunch Member

"*To Wendy's With Love* is about several generations of one family. Like many families, things have gone unsaid and longtime secrets withheld. In the welcoming environment of 'their' Wendy's, unspoken hurts and feelings emerge, resolving differences and pulling the family ever closer. Perhaps that's what we all need—a commitment to spend time together, eat lunch in a comfortable spot and talk. We can all benefit from reading this touching memoir."
—Merle Minda, Writer and Columnist

"It's wonderful knowing that in a world where good service and hospitality are fast disappearing, it's still alive at Wendy's. Sign me up. Who wouldn't want what Diane and her family have found there?"
—Pamela Muldoon, Muldoon Media, Content Marketing Institute

"Diane Keyes' memoir, *To Wendy's With Love,* is a beautiful testimonial to loving the moment and the family we're in. This poignant and touching story will make you both laugh and cry as the lunch bunch relationships multiply and deepen with the passing months and years. I'd love to be in the Keyes/Andersen family!"

—Gloria VanDemmeltraadt, Author of *Musing and Munching.*

Also by Diane Keyes

Spirit of the Snowpeople
This Sold House

to Wendy's with Love

the 22-year lunch

Diane Keyes

Third Child Press

2017

©2017 Diane Keyes. All rights reserved.

Published by Third Child Press
www.thirdchildpress.com

ISBN: 978-0-9767999-4-8

First edition
05 04 03 02 01 11 12 13 14 15

Publisher's Cataloging-in-Publication
Names: Keyes, Diane.
Title: To Wendy's With Love : the 22-year lunch / Diane Keyes.
Description: Minneapolis : Third Child Press, 2017.
Identifiers: LCCN 2010935234 | ISBN 978-0-9767999-4-8 (pbk.) | ISBN 978-09767999-5-5 (Kindle ebook)
Subjects: LCSH: Food—Social aspects. | Family life. | Self-actualization (Psychology) | Women—Biography. | Autobiography. | BISAC: BIOGRAPHY & AUTOBIOGRAPHY / Personal Memoirs. | BODY, MIND & SPIRIT / Inspiration & Personal Growth.
Classification: LCC GT2850 .K49 2016 (print) | LCC GT2850 (ebook) | DDC 394.125—dc23.

Cover Design by Shannon Lindquist-Dulin
Interior Design by Sue Stein

Dedication

To my mother, Lorraine Andersen,
to Wendy's own Dave Thomas,
and to Mike Givens,
the owner of our local Wendy's restaurants—
all founders of the feast.

Acknowledgments

Writing this book has made me profoundly thankful for every encounter, person and crisis that has been, or will ever be, part of my life story.

Many people are responsible for the creation of this book. When I joined WOW, my writers group, there were twelve of us, now, 15 years later, 220 women call themselves Women of Words. I have been blessed to learn so much from so many. Your friendship, help and support is my motivation—I want you ALL to be proud of me. To Connie Anderson, Colleen Szot, Mary O'Keefe, Merle Minda, and Laura Barclay: *thank you* is simply not a big enough word. And to Roshini Rajkumar and Wendy Neuman—your BIG plans for this book helped me realize my dreams, I am richly blessed and profoundly grateful to you both.

To my Book Marketing Roundtable friends, led by the heroic and hilarious Kristen Brown: Thank you for reenergizing my interest in the Wendy's project after years of starts and stops.

To our Wendy's family in Minnesota, Linda, Mike, and Michael Givens, as well as Sarvat and Jacquie, who have served us so well, without your loving attention to our family, this book would not have been written.

To the wonderful people at the Wendy's corporation: Emil Brolick, Liliana Esposito, and Bry Roth, who have been so kind and encouraging to us…we are deeply grateful. And finally to my family and friends, I may have written down the words, but you ARE the Wendy's story.

Table of Contents

Foreword		1
Introduction		3
Chapter One	If These Chairs Could Talk	5
Chapter Two	Secrets, Silence—and Change	9
Chapter Three	Old Baggage and New Beginnings	27
Chapter Four	Grace on a Bun	49
Chapter Five	The Strength to Suffice	65
Chapter Six	The Lunch Bunch Regulars	73
Chapter Seven	A Golden Thread	103
Chapter Eight	A Happy Accident	113
Chapter Nine	Where's The Beef?	125
Chapter Ten	Returning to the Table	129
Chapter Eleven	It *Is* a Wonderful Life	135
Epilogue	The Rest of the Story	143

Foreword

We, at Wendy's FourCrown Inc., are delighted and honored to be the subject of award-winning author Diane Keyes' memoir, *To Wendy's With Love*. It is our mission in each restaurant to strive for a family dining experience that inspires the loyalty and affection that the Keyes/Andersen family feels for their own Wendy's in Roseville, Minnesota.

We are pleased to promote and support *To Wendy's With Love* as the epitome of our values here at FourCrown. It is our fondest wish that you will find the same warmth, hospitality and family connection this family has found—and it will bring you back to us and each other, week after week, year after year.

> The Mike and Linda Givens Family
> Owners of Wendy's FourCrown Inc.

Introduction

The Universe has a way of weaving the disparate threads of our experience together to create the works of art we call our lives. So here I am, writing a book I could never have imagined twenty-two years ago, about our family's weekly gatherings at a fast-food restaurant, and how those get-togethers have changed my life.

For years I've been telling everyone who would listen about our lunch bunch at Wendy's. Many of them said, "Diane, you are a writer, this is a great story. Write a book." But sometimes things aren't as simple as they seem on the surface.

It's hard to be honest, especially on paper, about my relationship with my parents. I don't want to risk hurting my mom, whom I adore, or my dad's memory, which I cherish.

However, I've come to understand risk is part of life, and I reached the conclusion, with the encouragement of friends, that this book is a tribute to my parents, and a triumph for the happiness and well-being of families everywhere.

I commit these words to paper, in the hope many lives will be enriched and many hearts will be healed, as you find possibilities for your own families between the lines of our story. It could be your story, too.

Chapter One

If These Chairs Could Talk

And suddenly you know: It's time to start something new and trust the magic of new beginnings.—Meister Eckhart

It seemed like an ordinary day. No banners in the sky, no celestial choir heralding the good news, and no evidence to indicate one little question that impulsively popped out of my mouth was going to change the course of my life. At age forty-five, I was finally about to grow up.

"Should we go to lunch *every* Thursday?" I asked my mother after we'd lunched together successfully two weeks in a row. Much to my surprise and delight, Mom did not hesitate. "Yes, I'd like that. I'll have to call the girls to tell them we'll need to move our bridge game to Fridays—but that's okay. They can't play without me.

"Where should we go, Diane? It needs to be close, affordable, and their menu needs to have some variety. Fran won't come if we do Mexican every week so that's out. What about Wendy's? They serve chili as well as burgers, salads, and baked potatoes. And I do love their Frosties. Besides, it will make things a lot easier to go to the same place all the time."

"That's fine with me, Mom. Wendy's it is." Off we went, unaware of the tradition we had so casually put in place. Who could have guessed we would still be meeting at the same place every week, collecting the unexpected benefits that have accrued from our trivial choice nearly *1,100 lunches and 22 years ago?*

Like the blueprint for a new building, we'd discovered a plan for becoming more than just a good-time, holiday kind of family—we were building a new foundation, week by week. Early on, it was the three of us: Mom, my Aunt Fran, and me. However, as weeks turned into months, and months into years, word of our little lunch bunch spread, and soon it was not unusual to have ten, twelve, or even sixteen family members and friends join us.

However, this is much more than a story about the number of hamburgers, fries, bowls of chili, and Frosties consumed in those twenty years, although the numbers are staggering. It's about the people—those who have come, and those who have gone; the ones who moved away, and the ones who went to heaven. All of them left their mark on us and are deeply missed now that their chairs are empty. These gatherings have filled us up, individually, and as a family, every week for all these years, changing us, stretching us, surprising us, and enriching our lives in ways we never imagined.

This book may be about my family, but if you look closer and dig deeper, you'll also find your own family here. Meeting around the table, regardless of where it is, and who shows up, is what counts. It is together at the table that our stories come to life, our burdens are shared, our joys are multiplied, old memories find new meaning, and new memories are made.

Welcome to lunch at Wendy's. We're delighted to have you join us. Pull up a chair and sit down.

Small cheer and great welcome makes a merry feast.
—William Shakespeare

Chapter Two

Secrets, Silence—and Change

Nobody can go back and start a new beginning, but anyone can start today and make a new ending. —Maria Robinson

In the more than 1,100 times we've gathered at Wendy's, we've shared lots of fun and laughter. But the real story behind this simple little event is about change, the capital "C" kind of change eating lunch together one day a week has made in our family, especially in me.

At the age of eight, in August of 1955, a brain hemorrhage stole my childhood from me, along with the sense of safety and security I had taken for granted. Because I was a child, I did not understand that although my parents loved me, they could not protect me from the adversities of life. Nor did I realize that, like most parents of their generation, my mother and father did not believe it was appropriate to discuss such adult topics with me. The loneliness I felt being left without answers, and the terror of my experience, created an empty well of isolation, fear, and frustration in me I did not understand—and my parents could not fill.

Regrettably, it took many years for me to come to terms with my childhood feelings, and longer still *to let them go*. An ever-present sense of perceived loss permeated my relationship with my parents because I carried those unmet needs into every conversation and circumstance for the next thirty-seven years of my life. Fortunately for all of us, our weekly lunches at Wendy's began to fill my soul with a wellspring of healing and love, which soon engulfed our entire family.

Before sharing how our Wendy's lunches came to be, and what they mean to all of us, it helps to understand how far we've come. And so I must go back to the beginning, at least as far back as living memory allows.

It's a familiar story; one played out the world over by families in poverty and prosperity, in mud huts and mansions, ever since Eve first loved Adam…

More than a hundred and twenty years ago, in a small

town near the backwaters of Lake Superior, a baby girl was born. Raised to be an obedient, chaste girl with high morals, strong principles, and a fear of God, she grew into a beautiful young woman. Many young men asked for her hand, but Ethel's heart beat for just one boy, the eldest son of the deputy police chief.

Henry was kind, friendly, popular, and very good-looking. Although many girls had a crush on him, he spent most of his time after school caring for his younger brothers and sisters, and Ethel thought there was little chance he would ever notice her.

Upon graduating high school, Ethel went to work in the paper mill offices. Much to her delight, so did Henry. Eventually, he did notice her and fell as deeply in love with her as she was with him, vowing to make her his own.

Unfortunately, as they often do, outside events interfered with their plans. In the fall of 1912, Henry's father was offered a good job in Chicago, and since their family was large, and wages were higher in a big city, he accepted. Because Henry's parents relied upon their eldest son to care for his siblings and help support the family, he had no choice but to move with them to Illinois. And so, although they'd previously shared only chaste kisses and innocent embraces, desperately afraid of losing Henry, Ethel gave him her most precious gift, and he whispered earnest promises.

By the time Ethel discovered she was pregnant, Henry was gone. Confident of his love for her, she immediately wrote to him in Chicago. However, unbeknownst to her, on their way through Illinois, an old friend of Henry's parents offered his father a good job as the chief of police in his small town. Having had second thoughts about living in such a large city, his parents decided to accept their friend's kind offer, and make their new home in Rock River, Illinois.

Ethel waited patiently for a reply, but her urgent message never reached him. Once fresh and bright with promise, her future with Henry seemed as faded and brittle as the wildflowers he'd given her on their last day together.

Unaware Henry had not received her letter, and too hurt and proud to write again, Ethel saw no other choice but to tell her mother. Shocked by her daughter's revelation, but determined to find a way to handle the situation discreetly, her mother advised her not to tell anyone about her pregnancy.

That night as she lay in bed, Ethel heard her parents in their room next door arguing about her fate. Pulling the quilt over her head, she tried to muffle the sting of their words—words filled with sorrow and rage, failure and frustration, dis-

Secrets, Silence—and Change

appointment and resentment—words which would echo in her head years later when sleep refused to offer its respite.

Within days, her mother came to her with the arrangements in place. Ethel would leave home, ostensibly for a new job, to live with her father's parents in Stillwater until the baby was born. Then she would return home with the baby, and her mother and father would raise the infant as their own.

The plans were set in stone; she had no say in the matter. At any other time in her life, the spirited Ethel might have fought for another solution, but despondent over Henry's desertion she had no fight left—no answers other than those her mother provided. With her heart broken, and her hopes dashed, she rode to the train station with her father, his silence more painful than any blow, more humiliating than any words.

And Henry? When he tried to contact Ethel, her father told him she had left town and had asked that he not try to contact her again. Unaware of what was actually happening to Ethel, Henry soon forgot the girl back home in favor of the girl next door.

Ethel's confinement passed slowly, with only her work at her grandparents' grocery store as diversion. Her grandparents made no mention of her condition. Their denial was so absolute sometimes she would be taken aback when she caught her reflection in a window glass.

But when she felt the child quicken in her womb, she rejoiced. The new life she and Henry had created was her only connection to him, and she loved this child with all her heart. She spent long hours alone in her room, talking to her baby and making plans for them. When the time came to give birth, her grandmother helped Ethel deliver her precious Pearl.

Knowing Pearl's challenging circumstances, God gave her a bit more of everything that makes a child irresistible—and she was. With a beautiful halo of blonde hair and compelling blue eyes, which reflected the glory of her heavenly home, her smile captivated everyone who saw her. And on her sweet face nestled a perfect little dimple, marking the spot where God Himself had kissed Pearl farewell on her way into the world.

Renewed by her daughter's tender presence, Ethel resolved to claim the child for her own, and to stand against the recriminations and judgments she knew would come. As soon as she was able, the two of them boarded the train for home.

Ethel's nervous parents met them at the station, uncertain about their feelings for the child. However, by the time they arrived home, Pearl had melted her grandparents' hearts. Their ready acceptance of the baby gave Ethel the courage to

Secrets, Silence—and Change

speak her mind. But before she could say a word, her mother began laying out the plan she'd already put in motion. She had told her friends she and her husband were adopting a baby they'd named Helen. Since the adoption was taking place in Minneapolis, when Ethel moved back home, she would be bringing her new "little sister" with her.

Ethel was stunned. "Pearl is my baby, not yours. I thought I could give her up, but I can't. She is mine. I will not let you take her from me."

Her mother continued. "We're not taking Helen from you. Your father and I are giving you both your only chance for respectable lives. You know how people talk. Your father and I will love and care for her as our very own. You can stay here too, close to Helen, and be the best big sister any little girl ever had. And when you marry, Helen can visit often and even spend summers with you. It will work out, you'll see."

Looking to her father for help, Ethel watched him raise the newspaper to keep her sad eyes from penetrating his breaking heart.

"It's Pearl, her name is Pearl," Ethel cried. Snatching the baby from her mother's arms, she ran up the stairs to her room, slamming the door.

Over the next few days, Ethel tried to change her mother's

mind, but to no avail. Although she listened to her daughter's pleas, she would not be swayed. In the end, Ethel knew it was futile to argue any longer. She needed the help her parents were offering, such as it was. She had only one hope: if the church stood behind her, her mother would yield to her faith. Their pastor, Father Ryan, would make her mother understand, she was sure of it.

The following morning Ethel rose early, bundled up the baby, and took her to Mass. After the service, she asked to speak privately with Father Ryan. She explained her situation as calmly as she could, and then recounted her mother's unreasonable solution.

"My dear girl, you're to be commended for wanting to take responsibility for your baby," Father Ryan began, gently taking her hand. Ethel took heart, but only for an instant. "Nevertheless, you must see how impossible the situation would be, child." Then he outlined the same arguments her mother had made, the very ones Ethel had tried to deny.

"Ethel, you did a courageous thing to bring Pearl into the world without a husband. You must continue to be brave and accept the help God is offering you through the generosity of your parents.

"You need to surrender to God the idea of yourself as her

Secrets, Silence—and Change 17

mother. From today forward, you must accept Helen as your sister—your mother's child. It is best for you and for your baby. Don't ever mention this again to anyone, as long as you live. And that includes Helen. Now go in peace, with God's blessing." Then he made the sign of the cross on both their foreheads, and escorted them to the door.

Beyond despair, Ethel walked through the alleys, away from prying eyes, towards a home she no longer saw as a refuge but as a prison. How could she give up Pearl?

But if Father Ryan agreed with her mother, it must be the right thing to do. She would find the strength and do what was best for her daughter. She would make the sacrifice and learn to live with it. In that moment, where desolation met duty, Ethel made a solemn vow, to love Helen in the only way left to her, within the secret recesses of her heart. And a veil of sorrow descended upon her and stayed with her forever.

Relieved at Ethel's acquiescence, her mother urged her to stop breast-feeding Helen. Sad but resolute, Ethel severed her last remaining maternal bond.

Life went on, and soon she saw the light in Helen's eyes shine more brightly for her new mother than for her. It was to be expected. Ethel's mother doted on Helen, allowing Ethel to help only when absolutely necessary.

Although Ethel knew Helen was doing the only thing a helpless babe could do, the pain was too great. Despondent and defeated, she went back to her grandparents. Having done what they thought she should, she was welcomed with open arms, and returned to a quiet life working at the grocery store.

She soon found companionship with a young man she'd met during her previous stay in Stillwater. Knowing Fred knew about her child and still cared for her, Ethel felt safe with him. In his company, she was able to forget about her baby for hours at a time, and she loved him for that. As for Fred, it had been love at first sight, and his compassion for her plight made him love her even more.

Determined to make this lovely, but sad, girl happy again, Fred married her as soon as she said yes. Eleven months later, their daughter, Marion, was born. Ethel had everything she needed to be happy—everything, except Helen. She visited the child as often as possible and found comfort watching her children play together and grow to love each other. Still, it was not enough. The lies and untruths needed to keep the charade in place took a terrible toll on her.

Ethel knew her entire hometown was complicit in the secret. She could see it on their faces and in their gestures and

Secrets, Silence—and Change

whispers, whenever she came home to visit. But afraid of making things difficult for Helen, and determined to keep her promise to God and Father Ryan, she said nothing.

Although Fred knew the circumstances of Helen's birth, he could not scale the wall around Ethel's shame. Ethel believed she must carry her burden alone, shutting Fred out and remaining isolated in her misery. All Fred could do was love her and the girls as much as possible. And he did.

Another daughter was born to Ethel and Fred two years later. Best friends as well as sisters, Marion and little Frannie were inseparable. And they loved their "cousin" Helen like the sister she actually was.

During the fall of 1924, nine-year-old Marion came down with pneumonia. Without the money to pay for hospitalization, Ethel and Fred cared for her at home as best they could. One morning when they believed Marion was over the worst of it, Frannie went upstairs before school to say good-bye and give her sister a hug and a Slow Poke sucker.

Her eyes bright with fever, Marion pointed up at the ceiling and said, "It's okay Frannie, I won't need the sucker anymore. Look at all those sparkly bright flies, they're coming to get me. Aren't they beautiful?"

Terrified, Frannie ran downstairs screaming, "Ma, come

quick, the angels are coming for Marion." Grabbing her youngest daughter, Lorraine, from her high chair, Ethel flew up the stairs, but the angels had already taken her precious Marion.

Drowning in a sea of relatives and sympathy, Ethel snuck out of the house late that evening looking for peace and solace where she'd often found it, on the shores of a nearby lake. This time she found nothing but the echoes of her parents' harsh words from another dark night long ago, and the accusing laughter of the loons as they mocked her grief.

Though Ethel's pain was deep and raw, life moved on. She poured what was left of her heart into her four daughters—Frannie, Lorraine, and the two new baby girls, Phyllis and Dolores, who soon joined them. The birth and presence of each one a bittersweet blessing and a constant and painful reminder of the child she was forced to deny.

With her need for Helen greater than ever, Ethel's trips up north became more frequent and less discreet. When the town's busybody, Millie Frost, heartlessly teased her saying she should be happy to have *five* girls, Ethel could not resist some finger-pointing of her own. A cruel and vengeful person, Millie cornered twelve-year-old Helen as soon as Ethel left town, taunting her and insisting she was Ethel's illegitimate daughter, not her sister.

Secrets, Silence—and Change

Expecting firm reassurance and a passionate dismissal of Millie's claim, Helen ran home unprepared for her mother's words. "Helen, my sweet girl, you are the child of my heart," her mother said, stroking her hair gently. "Millie is a cruel person to say otherwise. Pay no attention to what other people say. And do not, under any circumstances, speak of this to your sister Ethel, it would hurt her terribly."

A bright, insightful child, Helen found the unwelcome truth and fuller meaning behind her mother's measured words, and in an instant grasped her past, present, and future. Like her mother and grandmother before her, Helen fell heir to the legacy of secrets and half-truths that haunted them.

Even though Ethel knew of Millie's betrayal, in the ninety-three years of her life, never did she acknowledge the child she loved beyond measure. Nor did Helen, in her own ninety-three years, ever claim her mother or sisters as her own. The secret inflicted a pain so strong it pierced the heart of each woman, changing forever who they might have been, yet so weak it would have vanished with a few words of truth spoken in love.

This is my Grandmother Ethel's story. Although I know only the barest facts about this early chapter of her life, I feel the truth of the telling in my heart. And I know with certainty she sat with me as I wrote, whispering her life into my pen and urging me on. I tell the story to honor her and, in some way I hope, redeem her suffering.

Even as a child, I recognized the pain in her eyes and heard it in her frequent sighs, although its source remained hidden. I knew of Marion's death, of course, but Grandma's sorrow seemed to surround her, casting a shadow over everything about her.

I remember how troubled my grandmother was when several students from my high school were killed in an accident on their way to bible camp. She paced the floor, rubbing her arms to keep away the cold death always brings with it. Seeing her distress I asked, "Are you thinking of Marion?" Her head sank deep into her shoulders as she nodded yes.

Fully aware I was treading on shaky ground, I murmured timidly, "How long has it been since her death." Without hesitation she replied, her voice raw as if the words themselves were shards of glass, "Forty-nine years, three months, and eighteen days." She paused, summoning the strength to utter what till now she'd only dared think. "The loons laughed the night Marion died."

Those words chilled me to the bone and told me time had not dulled the sharp edge of her sorrow. Her response was so

Secrets, Silence—and Change

visceral, her grief so fresh... her heart still lying broken on the shore. But when I reached out to comfort her, she had already disappeared behind the wall her secret had built.

Years later, when Helen's daughter shared her mother's story, my mind returned to that moment between my grandmother and me when, for an instant, she had allowed me to see the depth of her pain.

I think, in her grief and despair, my grandmother believed God took Marion to punish her for having a child out of wedlock. And so she mourned with equal intensity the two daughters who were both lost to her. Guilt and misplaced obedience holding hostage the sweet and comforting memories of little Marion, and depriving her of Helen, who alone could ease her suffering. And most grievous of all, stealing from her heart a belief in a forgiving and compassionate God.

The foundation for secrecy and silence that caused Ethel's torment, and my own, was already firmly in place generations before I was born, probably even before her birth. My grandmother's family, like many others, before and since, raised their children to strictly adhere to the "no-talk rule." This unspoken directive prevents honest communication both inside and outside the family, and fosters secret-keeping.

Although family members grow up believing loyalty demands they keep silent to protect the family, in reality the secrets stifle communication and undermine relationships. This disturbing cycle creates a climate where guilt, shame, anxiety, and depression can thrive—exacting an untold cost. John Bradshaw, noted psychologist and relationship expert, says in his book, *Family Secrets*, that even when a family secret is known by only one or two family members, the negative effects are still felt by the entire group.

My grandmother paid an incalculable price for remaining faithful to her family story. And, recognized as neither daughter nor sister, Helen, an innocent, paid just as dearly, as did her children. It is painful to even consider the rejection, slights, and omissions that Helen and her family must have faced with heartbreaking regularity all their lives.

Not knowing the truth, the rest of us forfeited the joy of deeper family ties, kindred memories, and common celebrations, as well as countless lost opportunities for closer connection.

Our history forms who we are and how we see ourselves, as individuals and as family. We can't learn from our history if we're not allowed to examine it honestly and bring it out of the shadows. Over the years, as I have shared this chapter of our family history with others. I've seen how many people carry the burden of similar secrets. It is my hope in recounting my grandmother's sad, yet common story, I can bring the destructive nature of secrets and silence into the light of present-day sensibilities. The time for such bondage is past.

What was once considered privacy is now recognized as dysfunction, which can be healed with open communication—and for our fortunate family, with one little lunch every week at Wendy's.

Then you will know the truth, and the truth will set you free.—John 8:32

Chapter Three

Old Baggage and New Beginnings

Be patient toward all that is unsolved...and try to love the questions themselves...Live the questions now.
—Rainer Maria Rilke

All families have their own stories of dysfunction. I'm convinced if one generation was fully functional, their children would still end up in therapy trying to figure out how to measure up to their parents' perfection. Nevertheless, each of us has a personal responsibility to learn from our own mistakes as well as those of past generations.

Many people say, "It's just the way I am," as if that statement alone is enough to excuse stubborn, narrow-minded, or simply unacceptable behavior. But more is expected from us. Without exception, every religious tradition, every faith, calls us to transcend our baser natures and become *more*—to reach for the dream of ourselves. I'm not talking about the platitudes heard at commencement speeches, like the quest for a better job, a bigger house, or a grander widget. I'm speaking about the only important quest: the journey to self-awareness, the journey within.

Ultimately, one of the most disappointing truths in life is that no matter whom you think it's about—it's about you. It's always easier, and more temporarily satisfying, to lay a problem at someone else's feet. Unfortunately, if you're honest with yourself, when you get right down to it, you find yourself and your own *stuff* at the core of every issue. Everyone looks for exceptions to the rule. I'm sorry to say there are none. I know; I've searched everywhere.

You think your husband should take out the trash *before* he hears the garbage truck coming. It's about you and your need to control the circumstances. You're angry because you are always available for your friend, but she is always too busy to help when you need her. It's about you and the expectations you have of others. You feel disappointed because your child won't go into the family business, which ensures financial se-

Old Baggage and New Beginnings 29

curity. Instead, he wants to open a non-profit center for abandoned animals, which you think has no chance of success. Surprise! It's still about you and your reluctance to accept reality. Your children are on the planet to do things *their* own way, *not yours.*

It's a frustrating lesson that needs to be learned again and again before it finally sticks. And frankly, I'm not sure it ever does stick. You'd think the concept would be easier to grasp, or you should remember it forever, after the hell you endured learning it the first time. But I've begun to think most of us are very limited in our ability to learn life's lessons, and apply them consistently.

Even though you peel away a layer of ignorance and learn a lesson in one instance, life lessons are like onions. There are plenty of them, and each one presents you with myriad opportunities to peel away its infinite layers in order to learn more about yourself at ever-deeper levels. And peeling them usually involves tears. No matter *whom* I think it's about, it's always about *me* and what I need to learn. It's the same for you, too. You must look inside for the answers.

This is my story. For the first eight-and-a-half years of my life, I was a happy, bright, and secure child. I had loving parents, devoted grandparents, and aunts and uncles who doted on me—the perfect recipe for an ideal childhood. But as we all know, things never stay perfect for very long.

My problems began in August of 1955, the month before I was to start fourth grade. It's easy to pinpoint the exact time because that's when I had a brain hemorrhage. The hemorrhage was, as they often are, the result of a congenital anomaly. At the time, before the advent of CAT scans and MRIs, they were described as birthmarks on the brain, small areas of weakened tissue on the surface of the vein or artery, ready to cause all kinds of havoc when they balloon out, burst, and bleed. Even today, brain hemorrhages are fatal for more than twenty-five percent of people who suffer from them. However, when I had mine in the 1950s, they killed nine out of ten victims.

That beautiful August morning, I was sitting on the sofa watching *Axel and His Dog,* a popular local children's TV show, and eating red licorice, a candy I haven't eaten since (no sense taking any chances), when I got a blinding headache.

My mom was downstairs doing laundry at the time. I tried to reach her, staggering to the basement door, across what instantly seemed like a much larger living room, bouncing off the sofa, end table, and hallway wall as I went. "Mom, Mom, come here. I need you," I yelled with my last bit of strength, right before my legs buckled beneath me. In the few seconds it took Mom to reach me, I passed out, and she scrambled to the phone for help.

I could hear her screaming out the back door to our next-door neighbors, "Ralph, Florence, come quick, help me, something has happened to Diane." They laid me gently on the bed and waited, for what must have seemed like an eternity, until the ambulance came. I remember feeling desperate to say *something*, but I couldn't speak, move a muscle, or open my eyes.

I don't recall anything more until I "woke up" to find myself looking down on me—the "physical" me—lying on an emergency room gurney, surrounded by several doctors working to save my life. Although it sounds like it must have been very scary, I had no sense of anxiety or fear, just the comforting knowledge my body was entirely separate from the "real" me. Even now, I can instantly bring to mind, with great clarity, the profound sense of well-being I experienced during the moments I spent in both worlds. This memory has been a comfort to me my entire life.

Hovering near the ceiling, I could see my mom frantically waiting in another room for news of my condition. I wanted to console her, tell her, "Mom, don't worry, I'm fine," but I instinctively knew I was simply an observer, unable to participate in what was happening.

God and our family doctor saved my life that morning. Dr. A. was my dad's bowling buddy, a member of our church, and also the doctor who delivered me. Living only a few blocks away from our home in Roseville, he arrived at the hospital even before the ambulance. A man of deep faith, he went to Mass every morning. His faith touched every aspect of his life, and on that day it touched mine as well.

As he raced to the emergency room, *something* inside him told Dr. A. that I needed a spinal tap. As soon as we arrived at the hospital, he performed the procedure, right then and there. This must have been the point when, close to death, the real "me" awakened to usher my eternal self to glory. I'm not sure what brought me back, though I've always thought it was, most likely, the sight of my mom and the anguish she so obviously felt at the thought of losing me.

I deeply believe in the power of prayer to change our hearts and bring the word of God close enough for us to hear. So it doesn't surprise me that someone like Dr. A, who took time from his hectic schedule each day to spend time in prayer and meditation, would have access to Divine wisdom.

Many years later, at my dad's funeral, Dr. A. told me he felt guided by the Holy Spirit to do the spinal tap on me. I have no doubt that is true. Nothing other than divine guidance could compel most physicians to take such extreme measures in the absence of any concrete evidence.

Dr. A's incredibly brave and rash decision relieved the pressure in my brain and saved my life that morning so many years ago. When I think of the risk he took for me, I am filled with awe at his dedication to his vocation, and a feeling of profound gratitude for the value he placed on my life. At that moment, saving me was more important to him than his own career. Today, in our litigious society, few physicians would risk the lawsuits that would inevitably result from such a dangerous and seemingly impulsive decision, even in the face of a patient's impending death.

Thanks to Dr. A's quick thinking, courage and faith, I completely recovered—physically, that is. But it took decades for me to fully recover emotionally. And even as I write these words, I'm not sure my healing is complete. Maybe few of us ever heal entirely from the trauma in our lives.

While I was hospitalized, I had several procedures. Every evening when my parents left my bedside, they'd say, "We love you, honey. We'll see you in the morning," and both of them would squeeze my hand in reassurance. In an effort not to frighten me, neither my parents nor any hospital staff told me about any upcoming "procedures." It wasn't until the nurse arrived in the morning to give me a pre-op shot that I got "the bad news." At which time she would say with a perky smile, "No, dear, you won't be having breakfast this morning, you're going to surgery." So instead of being scared some of the time, I was scared all the time.

I can still recall listening for the metal warming cover on the breakfast tray to clink on the juice glass when the aide left it outside my door. This comforting sound meant I was safe for another day, and could quit holding my breath. Icy fear slithered its way up my spine each time I heard a gurney coming down the hall towards my room, my heart pounding out the same staccato beat as its wobbly wheels. *Are you coming for me? Are you coming for me?*

An unspeakable fear grabbed hold of me then, and didn't let go for many years. It wasn't the heart-pounding kind of fear I felt in the hospital. Instead, a vague sense of dread kept me waiting, always waiting, for the other shoe to drop.

I had no fear of death—it left me the moment I knew my body was not *me*, but only a shell containing my spirit for as long as I needed it. It was a fear of life that became my constant companion, fear of the unknown: the unexpected twist that can be thrown at you in the blink of an eye, or comes for you on wobbly wheels.

It never fails to amaze me how you can be headed, with single-focused determination, in a certain direction one minute, and, in the next, an unforeseen event, phone call from your doctor, the police, or a family member, can change everything. What was, only seconds ago, your whole world, disappears in the face of something vastly more important—your whole *new* reality.

In a sense, that is exactly what happened to me. Nothing was the same after that August morning. The trajectory of my life changed the day the birthmark on my artery lost its battle to remain in place. My brain hemorrhage altered everything—how other kids saw me, how my family saw me—and most importantly, how I saw myself. I'm not sure I realized how much my illness changed things until I began writing this book.

Actually, I suppose it's not surprising that everyone treated me differently. Like Harry Potter, "I was the girl who lived." What happened to me was out of the ordinary, and no one, including my family, knew quite what to do, or what to expect from me. Rumors buzzed around me like bees. *Can Diane read, walk, or talk? Play tag, go swimming, ride a bicycle? Is she bald? Does she have a metal plate in her head? Does she look like a freak?*

No one brought up my "illness," except to ask how I was feeling, which was probably just as well since I didn't know anything about what happened to me. With the "no-talk" rule firmly in place, I didn't feel like I could ask any questions of my parents, and it never occurred to me to ask the doctor—not that he would have ever said anything without my parents' consent. For reasons I still cannot understand, I felt embarrassed, ashamed, and even guilty for what had happened. My fear was a big part of it too. I was afraid to ask questions because I was afraid to hear the answers—like my grandmother I was locked behind my own wall of shame, secrets, and guilt.

Although the questions on everyone's minds were never asked, their expressions spoke volumes as their eyes were magnetically drawn to the angry red scar on my neck. I'm sure they tried to look me in the eye, but they could not keep themselves from staring at the long incision. It was a very happy day for me when boys began looking at my breasts instead.

I felt different, too. As much as the entire experience changed me, it was the out-of-body experience more than anything that made me see myself differently. I went to Catholic school, and living only one block away from church, I attended Mass every morning. Like my classmates, by the tender age of eight, I'd memorized most of the Baltimore Catechism—the primer of my Catholic faith doctrine. However, until the hemorrhage, my faith had been just a word. Defined in the dictionary, faith means "belief without proof." My out-of-body experience gave me irrefutable proof, personal knowledge about the *eternal me*. But, as I'd learned to do, I also kept that very lonely secret to myself.

You may be thinking right now what happened to me probably took place in my imagination, in an anesthetically induced dream state. I wondered too. But God soon gave me proof that I hadn't imagined what I still remember so vividly.

While the eternal me was floating blissfully above my physical body, I'd noticed one of the physicians assisting with the surgery. In the 1950s, it was rare to see a woman doctor. A Korean woman doctor working in a hospital in St. Paul, Minnesota was as rare as, let's say, an out-of-body-experience. Small and soft-spoken, with a slight limp and a broad smile, I recognized her right away when she came into my room a few days after my first surgery. Her presence at my bedside assured me that my experience had been real.

I'd overheard enough people whispering outside my door to know that most people who had brain hemorrhages died. I'd received a great gift, but it was also a mixed blessing. Lying in my hospital bed, I had a lot of time to think about my near-death experience. After all, I was still alive.

Even as a child, it seemed reasonable to me to assume I had survived for a reason, and along with having lived came the responsibility to search for my life purpose. Why had my life been spared? This was a lot for an eight-year-old to carry. And living with that question changed me. Not just "a kid" anymore, I felt different, not better or worse, just different, apart. I was already on a spiritual quest.

Over the years, I've asked myself countless times, *Is this it? Is this the reason I was spared?* But I never felt with any certainty my search was over, until now. The mysteries, miracles and serendipities surrounding my life, our lunches at Wendy's, and the writing of this book, have given me the sense of purpose I've been seeking all my life.

Several years ago, I contracted a virus that gave me stomach-churning vertigo 24/7 for several months. In an effort to find the source of the problem, my doctor scheduled a CAT scan and, quite by accident, discovered an arteriovenous malformation (AVM) in my brain; the congenital defect that had caused the hemorrhage I'd had as a child. She told me, "The problem previously diagnosed as "a birthmark on your brain" is actually called an AVM, a condition which was un-

Old Baggage and New Beginnings

detectable in the 1950s. Although it's been dormant all these years, it is still as much a health risk to you now as it was when you were a child."

In the area of the brain where the vessels should look like a freeway, mine look like a bowl of spaghetti. Most of the time, AVMs remain undiscovered until they're discovered too late, in an autopsy. We've all heard stories of people who were talking on the phone, watching TV, or doing the dishes when they collapsed and died. When such sudden deaths occur, AVMs are often the culprit.

I'll never forget the phone call I received to tell me about my condition one dreary Friday afternoon in May of 1998. It was approximately three minutes before the doctors' office closed for the weekend. She began by mispronouncing my name. "Hello, Ms. Keys." (My name is *K-eyes*). "Your doctor is out sick today. I am calling to tell you that you have an AVM. And although I do not think you will die over the weekend, if you get a severe headache you should go to the emergency room immediately. Give us a call on Monday to schedule your brain surgery. Thank you Ms. Keys, have a good weekend."

When I interrupted her attempt to make a quick escape by asking what an AVM was, she said, "I do not know, that is not my area of expertise." Somehow, I was not surprised. It was clear her area of expertise was not tact or subtlety either. I guess her concession to bedside manners was telling me to have a good weekend.

As you might guess, I did not have a good weekend, but it sure was intense. Although I know I must have felt frightened, what I remember is feeling more angry than I'd ever felt in my life. I was outraged. It was impossible to imagine anyone thinking it was a good idea to call, pass on such "grave" information, and then leave me hanging over the weekend the way that nameless doctor did. It's one thing to die of an AVM, it's another to die because it's Saturday.

Insensitivity of such a monumental degree is, in itself, a valid reason for gun control. I don't believe in violence but…

Fortunately for her, instead of homicide, I chose to search the physicians' phone listings beginning with "A", looking for a neurosurgeon who could give me answers and listen to me vent—on a Saturday. My dialing finger was numb by the time I got to "G," where I found a wonderful doctor who listened respectfully and expressed sufficient outrage at the unconscionable behavior of a colleague. He assured me I would be fine for now, and told me to come see him on Monday.

Initially, he wanted to do the surgery as quickly as possible, but I guess I got a little cocky when I didn't die over the week-

Old Baggage and New Beginnings

end. Since the anticipated recovery for the surgery was six months, I asked, "Doctor, can you delay the surgery for several weeks? I'd like to attend a weeklong retreat in August. It's the final event of my three-year spiritual direction training program before I receive my certification." Reluctantly, he agreed. Little did I know how serendipitous my insistence on a delay would turn out to be.

While my husband and I waited for the surgery, we did our best to continue our normal lives. Tom went to the office every day, although it seemed to me he worked out of his home office more often than usual. I continued my job too—staging homes to help people sell their homes more quickly.

Lunch at Wendy's remained "a welcome bit of normal" each week, allowing my family to see that I was still okay, and keeping them in the loop about any medical updates, without making an announcement seem like an all-points bulletin. But try as we might, normal didn't always prevail. Sometimes adjustments needed to be made to accommodate our "new normal."

One day in particular, frightened and frustrated by a situation completely out of my control, I decided to walk off my anxiety under a bright sun and blue sky. I called to Tom in his office downstairs to let him know I was going, and walked out the door. After I'd gone a couple miles, I stooped down to retie my shoe and happened to glance behind me. There was Tom, following me in our car about a quarter of a mile down the road. He quickly pulled over trying to remain inconspicuous, but didn't quite manage it. In that instant, I realized as difficult as the situation was for me, it was just as tough for Tom. I walked back to him and said, "Honey, let's finish the walk together." As I said, life wasn't completely normal, but it wasn't all bad either. I fondly think back on that day and many others, recalling them with deep awe and profound gratitude for the loving care and concern I received during those long weeks of waiting.

On my way to a staging consultation one evening, distracted by the medical challenges ahead of me, I prayed I would be able to let go of my own concerns and focus on the needs of my client. After we'd staged everything but the living room, Karen, the homeowner, asked if I'd like to stop for a cup of coffee. As we chatted at her dining room table, I noticed a colorful painting hanging above the fireplace in the living room. Looking closer, I realized the eye-catching artwork was actually a highly detailed rendering of a human brain on the cover of a medical journal. Mug in hand, I wandered over to it, fully prepared to tell Karen that although it

Old Baggage and New Beginnings

was beautiful, it seemed somewhat unusual as a staging accessory. The words caught in my throat when I saw what was written in the fine print below—*A Depiction of an AVM*. The hair on the back of my neck stood on end as I blurted out, "Karen, I have an AVM."

"You do? I can't believe it. I'm a neurosurgeon. I work with the world's foremost expert on AVMs. He's located in Madison, Wisconsin. That's why I'm selling my house. I'm moving to Madison so Dr. M. and I can continue our research."

"Oh, my gosh. My nephew, Dave is getting married in Madison in two weeks. Tom and I are going to the wedding." We looked at each other, at first in speechless wonder, and then in uncontrolled laughter.

"Well," Karen said, regaining her composure and giving me a gentle hug. "We'd better get you an appointment with Dr. M. I'll call him in the morning."

Without Karen's help, I'd probably still be waiting to see Dr. M. Fortunately, she was able to make arrangements for a last-minute appointment. Amazingly, the day before Dave's wedding, Tom and I found ourselves sitting in Dr. M's office. After an in-depth discussion he said, "Diane, I've reviewed your records, seen the CAT, the angiogram, and the MRI. Unless you absolutely cannot live with uncertainty, I would advise you against having the surgery. It is extremely serious, with only a fifty percent chance of a successful outcome."

His descriptions of the other fifty percent of AVM patients…well, you really don't want to know. It was a no-brainer (I couldn't resist) to say with conviction, "Well, Dr. M., it's an easy call because there are no guarantees, life is *always* uncertain."

"Exactly," he replied, kissing me on the cheek, and sending us on our way. Needless to say, we skipped out the door, on our way to a celebration that had as much meaning to us as it did to our nephew and his lovely new bride.

As soon as we arrived home, I made an appointment to consult with the surgeon who was scheduled to perform the procedure. As we sat nervously waiting for him in a private conference room, we began anticipating what we were sure would be a very uncomfortable meeting. To put it simply, we were loaded for bear, expecting him to argue in favor of the surgery. After all, that's what neurosurgeons do—they cut. All of a sudden Tom took my hand and looked deeply into my eyes. "This isn't the way we should approach this discussion. Let's pray for our meeting to go well." And so we prayed for peaceful hearts.

Right after we finished our prayer, the doctor burst through the door. Barely in the room, with his hand still on the doorknob he said, "Diane, I've been reviewing your records again. I think we should cancel the surgery. It's just too risky. You've lived for forty years without incident. You've survived two pregnancies, labors, and deliveries. By all accounts, they should have killed you. Let's leave well enough alone."

"Amen!" we chorused. It was over, as suddenly as it had begun. It was a good decision—I'm still here.

While the surgery had been on the calendar, my mom and dad had been worried and upset. In preparation for the surgery, the doctors decided to do a cerebral angiogram to get a better look at what was going on. They'd also thought there was a chance they might be able to fix the defect without the other, more major operation. Always a little dicey (and a bit more so in my case because of some twisted veins), the procedure consisted of threading a catheter up through my body and into my head, using dye to produce images of the blood flow in my brain. Unfortunately, although they were able to refine their approach for the upcoming surgery, they were not able to eliminate the problem.

My parents had wanted to be with me for the angiogram, but selfishly, I'd asked them not to come because I wanted to keep the surgery from feeling like a major event. Nevertheless, when I awoke from the anesthesia, they were at my bedside.

In the end, I was glad they were there. I'd been wrong. Some of my feelings of isolation and loneliness began to heal in the recovery room when Mom and Dad held my hand after the angiogram—just like they had when I'd been in the hospital all those years ago. Healing made possible, in part, by our weekly Wendy's get-togethers, which, by that time, were playing such a big role in the blossoming of our relationship.

Until that afternoon, I'd always seen myself as the primary casualty of the hemorrhage. However, I realize now, I wasn't the only one wounded by the fallout from the bomb in my brain. The shock of nearly losing their little girl never left my parents.

In a rare moment of candor, Mom tearfully told me ever since that morning in August 1955, she's been afraid of losing me. On the day I had my hemorrhage, Mom began praying a novena to St. Jude, the patron saint of hopeless causes. The novena, a special prayer meant to be said on *nine* consecutive days, was a petition to God to save my life. My darling, devoted mother has continued saying that prayer every day for the past fifty-seven years, afraid if she stops I might die. It makes me want to cry when I think of the anxiety Mom has lived with in secret all these years.

Old Baggage and New Beginnings

Without question, my mother loved me then and loves me now. However, I suspect in an effort to escape the pain she felt at the thought of losing me, she unintentionally masked all her feelings to keep me from seeing her fear—and to emotionally protect herself. However, to me, an eight-year-old traumatized child, my mother's fear looked and felt like distance. Things might have been so different had I known.

Part of the reason I think I'd felt so alone was because my parents never talked to me about my brain hemorrhage, and what had happened to me. For many families and cultures, the prevailing wisdom of the day was: "Don't rock the boat." "Let sleeping dogs lie." "Mind your own business." In other words, "Don't talk about it."

In the '50s, it was not considered appropriate to include children in discussions about serious matters. As a result, my parents did what they thought was best for me. They closed the door on that chapter of my life. Unfortunately, we were on opposite sides of the door.

I felt confused, scared, and profoundly alone. As I reflect on those feelings now, I realize, buried under the fear, confusion, and powerlessness, I must have been angry, not on a conscious level, but on a deep primal level, one affecting my entire view of the world. That little eight-year-old girl needed an explanation, and she needed reassurance and consolation. Instead she was left to deal with those feelings on her own—*and she wasn't very good at it.*

Eventually all those unresolved feelings came out sideways, in an against-ness towards any authority and especially towards my parents, primarily my mom. This made me difficult to live with, and caused me to respond negatively to almost everything they suggested, recommended, or endorsed. I grew older—but I didn't grow up. The frightened and angry eight-year-old inside me continued to call all the shots.

They say if you don't heal it, it's still a new wound. So I suppose it's not surprising that I brought a lot of baggage with me into adulthood and beyond. And that's what I was carrying through the door when grace entered my life, by way of a fast-food restaurant, the day I went to lunch with my mother for the first time.

The day we finally began talking—*and I began healing.*

The only journey is the journey within.
—Rainer Maria Rilke

Chapter Four

Grace on a Bun

I do not at all understand the mystery of grace—only that it meets us where we are but does not leave us where it found us.—Anne Lamott

The closer I got to my parents' home, the slower I drove. One foot on the brake, one on the gas, driving the same way I lived, going nowhere. The years I spent endlessly searching for the reason I felt the way I did about my family, my mother, and my life, had yielded no answers, only more frustration. As the car neared the corner of their street, my heart raced, the steering wheel grew slippery in my sweaty grasp, and I turned in the opposite direction, toward the safety of my own home.

Again and again, my faulty GPS took me home. When I did screw up my courage and stopped to see Mom and Dad, I often left feeling upset, but didn't know why. Never one to play favorites, I didn't reserve this behavior just for my family either. I cancelled plans with my friends almost as often as I made them. An introvert on my best days, I made the reclusive Howard Hughes look like a real party boy. Days went by, sometimes a week, without my leaving the house or even getting dressed. I managed to keep the house clean and make the meals, but everything was a struggle.

At age forty-five, after thirty-seven years of grief, confusion, and what I now recognize as depression, I'd grown weary of the status quo. I was tired of feeling angry and upset all the time; I was tired of me.

It is often said that nothing changes until something changes. And even then, change only occurs when it is too painful to remain the same. On a pain tolerance scale of one through ten, I'd stepped off the scale, way off. My life had become intolerable. It was time for a change.

Marianne Williamson, spiritual activist and author, says, "The only thing lacking in any situation is that which you are withholding." Regrettably, this had been true for me. For years, I'd withheld plenty, even my actual presence.

And that's exactly where I found myself one Thursday morning when I screwed up my courage, pulled in the driveway, and asked Mom to go out for lunch. It didn't feel like an inspiration, it felt more like desperation. I badly needed something to change. In that moment, I was given what seemed like a simple answer—an effortless way to spend time with my mom. Twenty-plus years later, I know it was grace.

The first week we talked about nothing in particular at lunch. It was a glorious September day. The sun was warm, and the leaves, startled by the crisp air into their first blush of fall color, provided enough material to keep us talking for a solid hour. We laughed. It was wonderful. When I left, we hugged and both said, "Let's do this again."

I left Mom feeling euphoric. When Tom saw me that evening and asked about my day, I was so happy and excited I couldn't talk fast enough. I don't quite recall what I said, but I interrupted myself to say, "I'll be right back, I've got to call Mom." I eagerly raced to the phone and called Mom to ask if she'd like to go to lunch again the next week. Mom said yes.

It was another beautiful day, and we enjoyed another golden hour together. We were on our way. Although this may not seem like a big deal, it was an enormous first step for me. At the time, I was careful to avoid any situation I thought might set me off, and almost anything could. I don't mean I would fly into a rage—that rarely happened. However, I negatively interpreted almost everything my parents said to me. I was in such a dark place, saying "pass the salt" could send me over the edge.

It's no wonder. I know now, in an unconscious way, I was always anxious, quite likely a victim of Post-Traumatic Stress Disorder (PTSD). I was still listening for the sound of the gurney in the hospital corridor like I had when I was eight. In the past, I'd often left Mom and Dad's house, gnawing on every word they said, like a dog with a bone, until I made myself completely miserable. In reality, something was actually gnawing at me.

Although I did not understand my feelings at the time, I did realize my attitude and behavior were destructive. A part of me still said, "You've had a couple successful lunches with Mom, and picked up some brownie points. This can't possibly last. Quit while you're ahead." At that point in my recovery, it was still a major decision to get dressed in the morning, and the dark phantom of depression called to me. Fortunately, I ignored the beckoning shadows. I didn't quit. Grace prevailed.

I've thought long and hard about what made our first lunch together different. I know desire played a part because

I truly did want things to change. And grace certainly gave me the fortitude to continue. But something else entered my life along with grace. It was gratitude.

The moment grace opened the door, gratitude found its way into my heart.

The dictionary says "gratitude, thankfulness, or appreciation is a positive emotion or attitude in acknowledgment of a benefit one has received or will receive." After our first beautiful Thursday together, I *was* grateful, *and* thankful, *and* appreciative because I was able to *feel* grateful, *and* thankful, *and* appreciative for one successful lunch.

Finally, I could look at the bigger picture. My feelings weren't all about me. Instead of whining, complaining, and worrying about what I didn't have, I began to celebrate what I did have: the simple joy of lunch with my mother.

The following week when Mom and I decided to go to lunch again, Mom was just as eager as I was. Two weeks in a row, and not one problem had surfaced, no angry thoughts, no pouting, no bone chewing. It was amazing—even miraculous. It had been such a long time since I'd allowed myself to enjoy or appreciate *anything*.

The burdens I'd carried since childhood began to fall away as the comfort of gratitude found a willing home in me.

By this time, lunch included my mother's sister, Fran, since Mom washed and set Fran's hair every Thursday morning. My favorite aunt, godmother, and the life of every party, Fran was a little Archie Bunker and a little Joan Rivers, thoroughly entertaining and always unpredictable.

Although she and my mom were very close, they were as different as two people could be. You might say Fran was the total antithesis of her sister Lorraine. Where my mother is respectful, Fran was irreverent. Where my mother is refined, Fran was bawdy. Where Mom is careful, Fran was careless. Constantly embarrassed by Fran's direct and somewhat cheeky approach to life (my mother takes a more circuitous route), Mom did a lot of eye rolling. Still, she loved Fran just the same, and would have never considered going to lunch without her.

For my part, I got a huge kick out of Fran, and was delighted to have her join us. What I loved about Fran was she told the truth, uncensored, uncut, and often unwelcome. More a subscriber to the "no s**t rule" than the "no-talk rule," Fran was a rule-breaker, the one who helped forge the way for open communication. In any case, I figured she would head off any problems if I got myself into trouble, or she would cause enough trouble herself to take the focus off me. Either way, having her along seemed like a good idea.

We didn't know at the time what a great decision choosing Wendy's would turn out to be. It was also close, about ten miles for me, only about a mile and a half for Mom and Fran. My mom lives in Roseville, Minnesota, or as the rest of the family calls it, "the center of the universe." I suspect anywhere she lives would be the center of the universe for our clan. Seriously, if it isn't within a couple miles of her house, you probably can do without it.

I don't recall the details of our conversations the first year or so. Do you remember the episode of the *Seinfeld* show where Jerry and George come up with an idea for a TV show about nothing? Well, we were the Jerry Seinfeld show at Wendy's. We talked about recipes and the week's best coupon specials. We talked about our family, the kids, how good the chili tasted, or the most recent Vikings or Twins game. Mostly, we talked about nothing.

After a time though, as we grew more comfortable, Mom and Fran talked about their childhood, World War II, or my grandparents and great grandparents, and I would discover new things about my family. Hearing their stories helped me begin to see them as more than my relatives. Behind their roles they were individuals, with personal histories and experiences I knew nothing about.

One day when I walked into Wendy's with a basket of toys for our grandchildren to play with while we ate, Fran was reminded of something that happened during her time in the U.S. Army. I think of this story often now with so many military personnel returning from the Middle East.

Stationed in Norfolk, Virginia during the Second World War, one of Fran's assignments had been to meet the returning ships when they made port, and greet the troops coming home from the European theatre. It was her first day on this particular duty, and she did not know what to expect. She had already greeted several soldiers when she saw two men carrying a wicker laundry basket between them down the gangplank. As they moved closer, she saw the top of a man's head showing over the edge of the basket. All his limbs were missing. His name was Joe.

"Hey there, good looking, how would you like to go out dancing tonight," Joe quipped to Fran, with a heart-breaking smile. Her heart dropped to her feet as she stood her post. Stunned by the extent of his injuries, Fran had neither the time nor the tact to censor her response. "Well, soldier, I'm on duty tonight, how about tomorrow?" she bantered back. He laughed loud and long. Apparently, her reply was exactly what he needed to hear. They chatted for a few minutes before the soldiers went on their way.

Fran saw other men like Joe over the course of her duty, but Joe was the one she remembered and prayed for every day for the rest of her life. I think about Joe when I catch myself using the phrase "basket case." Fran told me the term was coined during the World War I to describe soldiers returning home in Joe's condition. Knowing Joe's story, somehow nothing in my life seems to warrant such an expression.

Another Thursday, when I said I was going to bring daisies to my friend, Connie, for her birthday, Mom quipped, "Just bring me French mints." I'd known for a long time she didn't enjoy flowers. Now for the first time I felt like I could ask why. It had always seemed such an unfriendly response to one of God's most beautiful creations. However, when she explained, I realized I would feel the same way if I shared her experience. Back in the day, as funeral tradition required, my grandparents had occasionally "waked" (held the reviewal/wake) deceased relatives in their living room. As she spoke, Mom buttoned her sweater against memory's chill. "The scent of funeral bouquets never left our front porch. To this day, I can still smell the stale aroma of dying flowers mixed with damp wood." Needless to say, her dislike of flowers no longer seems strange to me.

I've even learned things I didn't know about my own life. Recently, Mom shared something that, had I known at the time, might have lessened the trauma I felt from my brain hemorrhage. She told me both sets of my grandparents were so worried about me being frightened and alone when I was in the hospital, that even though it was a financial stretch for them, together they paid what was an enormous sum at the time to have a nurse stay with me all night, every night.

I still remember Gretchen, the nurse, sitting ramrod-straight on a chair next to my bed. She drew cartoon pictures for me and was very kind. Whenever I woke during the night, I'd see her sitting in the dark smiling at me, her profile outlined by the streetlight coming in through the window behind her. Assuming nurses sat in every room, I thought nothing of it. I had no way of knowing she was there especially for me. No one ever mentioned it.

I can't help wonder. Would I have wasted all those years being angry and depressed if I'd realized my grandparents brought her in to stay with me because they loved me so much, and wanted to make sure I felt safe? If I had known, I believe I would have seen Gretchen's vigil by my bedside differently, more like a guardian angel in a winged nurse's hat, serving as a standard-bearer for my family. Someone to protect me through the long, dark nights, reminding me I was loved and assuring me I was *not* alone. Instead, I simply accepted Gretchen's presence in a terrifying experience filled with dread, as the one person wearing a white uniform who didn't poke or prod me.

Since most of my trauma ultimately came from feeling isolated, I'm sure having such an evident sign of my family's love for me would have made a difference. However, I didn't know. And *not knowing came with a price—it always does.* I wish they'd told me, for so many reasons, not the least of which is that I would have loved to tell my sweet grandparents how much I appreciated what they did.

Stories, like the ones Mom and Fran shared, change your perspective. It's easier to find fault with people if you only see them one-dimensionally. When you complain about your boss to friends, it's because you see him just in his role as boss. You don't take into account that the kids in Little League think he's the best coach in the world. You don't realize that sometimes he's crabby at work because he always stays up with his little girl when she has a nightmare and can't go back to sleep. You don't know that he leaves love notes for his wife every day on the bathroom mirror, or that his beloved mother has cancer.

Learning more about Mom helped me to see her as the complete and wonderful woman she is, not just the single facet of her personality I identified as "my mother." Do you remember the old joke about the girl who goes to college, and can't believe how much her mother learned while she was away? Well, that was me. Discovering more about my mom's childhood, and seeing how those experiences shaped her life, helped me understand her in a way I never had before. I was deeply moved hearing the details of her nine-year-old sister's death when Mom was a toddler and Fran was only seven. Stories viewed through the lens of such a loss changed everything between us, just as my own loss had changed everything for me. I now had a context for understanding the woman, Lorraine, and the experiences that formed who she came to be.

Once I thought it was terribly disrespectful and inappropriate if someone used their parents' first names when speaking to, or about them. No more. Now I think it may be a good thing because using your parent's name creates a personal connection. Your parent becomes more of a person and less of an icon when you call him or her by name. Being an icon may foster respect, but it sure does get in the way of relationship.

With every lunch, my idea of 'Mom' grew. I began to see her as wife, daughter, sister, mother, and friend. In short, I began to see Lorraine Andersen was like me—wife, daughter, sister, mother, and friend. She was no more, no less. Wind-tossed by the storms of life, Mom was someone trying her very best to do the right thing, just like me, just like all of us.

When I began to see my mom differently, I began to see the world differently.

It's hard to believe a single hour a week at a fast-food restaurant could create such a tide of emotional ripples in my life and the lives of others. But it did. I could see the current changing before my eyes. Albert Einstein said, "There are two ways to live: you can live as if nothing is a miracle; you can live as if everything is a miracle." When I chose the latter, miracles appeared everywhere.

It was miraculous that after only a couple of weeks, Mom and I were both willing to commit to spend every Thursday having lunch together. It would have been easy to let other things get in the way, to make exceptions. To say, "I can't make it to lunch this week, I need a haircut," or "I promised my friend I'd see her, and Thursday is the only day I have available." When Mom told me she'd informed all her friends she was not going to be available to play bridge on Thursday anymore, I was surprised and pleased. My mom has lots of friends, and they are very important to her—but clearly I was too. The unspoken message was: We are putting our relationship and each other first.

I understand now my mom had often put me first, but until our weekly lunches, I don't think I'd ever put her first. At Wendy's, we came together as equals, both of us committed to setting aside this time exclusively for each other. We didn't sit down, have a heart-to-heart, and sign our names in blood—we simply met for lunch each and every week.

The next miracle was that I quickly realized something was different—and I knew what it was. Until Wendy's, having my husband, Tom, and two wonderful children, Kelsey and Troy, hadn't been enough to keep me from acting like a child again the minute I walked through my parents' front door. And it didn't stop with Mom waiting on me—getting me an iced tea or a piece of banana bread. As soon as we shifted into our *roles*, if Mom said anything resembling criticism—hinting that my hair was too long, my skirt was too short, or my blush was too heavy—I would pout like a five-year-old. Miraculously though, at Wendy's, we came together as equals. I was finally beginning to grow up and take responsibility for myself and my feelings.

Looking back, my childish attitude seems ridiculous. But I suspect this is not an uncommon phenomenon. When one person slips back into old familiar patterns of behavior, I guess it's not surprising the other person does too. Old habits are hard to break.

The world seems to fall neatly into two kinds of people—those who are comfortable with their old habits and roles, and those who aren't. One group enjoys attending their class reunions, and the other would rather chew tinfoil while listening to someone scratch their fingernails on a blackboard. I'm in the latter group. I believe I speak for my entire group when I say, "There is no going back, at least, not without consequences."

Being out to lunch with Mom, I could enjoy the relationship without the fallout triggered by our customary roles. Who'd have thought sitting down together for a junior cheeseburger and a Frosty would help level the playing field?

The unthankful heart...discovers no mercies; but let the thankful heart sweep through the day and, as the magnet finds the iron, so it will find, in every hour, some heavenly blessings!—Henry Ward Beecher

Chapter Five

The Strength to Suffice

No one saves us but ourselves. No one can and no one may. We ourselves must walk the path."—Buddha

My childhood brain hemorrhage was not the first time my mother had to face living with uncertainty. Like many women of the "greatest generation," Mom developed her strength and resiliency early on in life as a war bride.

My dad was in the U.S. Army when they married in the vestibule of St. Andrew's Catholic Church in Saint Paul, Minnesota, the Saturday before Easter in 1944. It was an unplanned wedding; Dad had been able to finagle a last-minute leave before he was scheduled to report for additional training at Fort Bragg, after which he was to be shipped out. Within a few short weeks of their wedding, my father was gone, and my mother was left behind to fend for herself.

Every so often, in nostalgic moments, like when a World War II-era song such as "I'll Be Seeing You," "Stardust," or "I'll Never Smile Again," is played on the radio, I will see a look on Mom's face and in her eyes that tells me she is young once again and with the man she loves. On those occasions, glancing over my shoulder into the past, she has shared snippets about her life when Dad was overseas. Once she told me, "I'm sure it's hard for you to imagine, but the country was on such high alert, and national security was so tight, I never even knew where Gordie was until he had moved to another location."

I don't wish to discount the pain, suffering, and worry today's military families endure while their sons and daughters, fathers and husbands, mothers and wives, are gone. But today they are able to communicate on a regular basis and can occasionally talk to and even see each other using Skype and Facetime. During WWII, military wives and families went for months, sometimes even years, without any word from their loved ones, or news about their condition or location.

Not knowing from day to day whether Dad was alive or dead must have been agonizing. But Mom has a pragmatic, even romantic view about it. "Every day we lived with doubt, and questions for which there were no answers. Yes, it was difficult not knowing what was happening, but virtually everyone was in the same boat. And everything in the country—the music, the conversation, the daily news, and even the movies—supported and affirmed my love, my loneliness, and my contribution to the war effort. We found great comfort in each other, in not being alone."

"And," Mom said, her eyes twinkling, "Although any letters I did receive were always heavily edited to keep from revealing what could be an intelligence leak, Gordie and I did manage to find some creative ways around the editing, despite the restrictions."

For as long as I can remember, every time Dad gave Mom a card or even wrote her a note, he would sign it with a combination of symbols and letters, and they always made Mom smile. I was curious, but when I asked about them, she said, "They are something private between us." It makes me happy to think of the secrets they've shared. Some secrets are sweeter kept.

Left on her own, my mom became the most competent and self-sufficient person I know. I think she had to be, to pass the long months while Dad was away. Working in retail to support herself, she modeled for a local department store, finding the time to become a flawless housekeeper, an excellent cook, and a great money manager in the meantime.

Not only competent, my mother is also a model of efficiency. When she cleans up after a meal, it's like watching a beautifully choreographed dance. She moves gracefully from sink to stove to refrigerator with no wasted movements. She never rushes around like a crazy person; she moves continuously, shifting from one task to another without dread or procrastination, and seemingly, without effort.

Most likely, an element of Obsessive/Compulsive Disorder (OCD) in our gene pool helps the cause and explains her getting up in the middle of dinner to wash fingerprints off the glass in the back door. But as my sister-in-law says, "Never has dysfunction worked as well for anyone as it does for Lorraine." And it's hard to disagree since she seems to have more free time than the rest of us put together.

But my mother's desire for order has never compromised her willingness to adapt to life's challenges with grace. When Dad died suddenly, not long after their fifty-fifth anniversary, I could see her heart was broken, but she bravely faced what needed to be done in the same capable way she always had. I watched her build a new life for herself, always honoring her life with Dad. Nevertheless, she moved forward with determination, courage, and a strong desire to find joy in the time remaining.

She taught me a lot about fortitude that first year after Dad's death. Many times she said yes when I'm sure she would rather have said no. I was awed by her absolute resolve to delight in life's continuing gifts. I watched with admiration when she allowed her grandchildren to talk her into riding on the back gate of a pickup with them, taking a ride on a Harley, and speeding down the alpine slide on Lutsen Mountain—something I'm too chicken to do. If pictures are worth a thousand words, her photo album is a testament to the resiliency of the human spirit.

When I asked her how she managed go on so bravely without Dad, she said, "No amount of wishing is going to bring him back, and since I'm still here, it's up to me to make the best of it." No self-pity, no regret, instead an honest acceptance of the cards she's been dealt and a willingness to face life—no matter how difficult. It's something she'd been preparing for since the day long ago when Dad left his own "Sweet Lorraine," to fight for his country.

An excellent athlete, Mom played on both golf and bowling teams until, at eighty-three, a rare muscle disease called polymyositis sidelined her. Within weeks, she was forced to move from the home she and Dad shared for nearly fifty years—a house she said she'd never leave. Nevertheless, she made up her mind quickly, and in the space of five days, she bought into a senior co-op building and sold her home.

Mom has made a great success out of her new life. She's made new friends; going to daily exercise classes, playing bridge, and joining all the activities. She delights in saying, "My co-op is actually more like a luxury cruise ship—the only thing missing is the water and the Lido deck." Nearly every day, she tells me how happy she is there.

While some of her ability to face life's challenges may be due to her willingness to adapt to life's changes, a lot can be attributed to her indomitable faith, which is as much a part of her life as the air she breathes. My mom is Catholic through and through.

When she married my dad, he was Lutheran. Mom never asked him to leave his church, she simply said, "You can go to your church, my church, or any other church you want to attend on Sunday, but you're not going to lie in bed while I go to church." It didn't take long for him to begin attending her church. About twenty years after they married, he converted to Catholicism. It turned out to be disappointingly anti-climactic though, since when they went to announce the big news, they discovered everyone assumed Dad was already Catholic because he never missed Mass on Sunday or holy days. Whether he went with her or without her, he never stayed in bed.

Beautiful inside and out, Mom's lasting beauty is just as compelling today as it was when she was young. As strong as she is beautiful, I think my mom's ability to accept life and be grateful for whatever comes her way, allows her beauty to shine through, despite any difficult circumstances.

When we celebrated my mother's 90th birthday in 2012, I realized I'm not alone in recognizing and honoring her resolute spirit. While we were making plans for the party, and discussing how many people we thought would attend, my sister-in-law, Katie said, "I don't know, but we'd better plan BIG. In the past, whenever, we've had anything for Lorraine, everyone comes." Katie was right; everyone did come. In fact, the crowd was too big to get an accurate count. Mom received over one hundred twenty-five cards at the party, plus all those the postal carrier delivered to her door every day for weeks.

Today, Mom is my inspiration. It fills me with joy to be able to see it, mean it, and say it. For too many years, my pain wouldn't allow me to see the truth. Happily, lunch at Wendy's helped change that, too.

Grace isn't a little prayer you chant before receiving a meal. It's a way to live.—Jaqueline Winspear

Chapter Six

The Lunch Bunch Regulars

Treat your family like friends, and your friends like family.
—Proverbs

My Own Dear Tom

Tom is the finest man I know. We met in third grade, began dating in high school, and married at the end of our junior year in college. He is sweet, smart, incredibly accomplished, consistently kind, and unbelievably honest.

Some years ago, he took a Minnesota Multiphasic Personality Inventory (MMPI) exam as part of a job interview. It was several weeks before they finally called him in to give him the results. The psychologist told Tom it took so long because he had asked six of his colleagues to go over the test results. He thought Tom was the first person to have cracked the code and snowed the exam. The real reason turned out to be that they simply did not know how to account for his extraordinary honesty.

I am a better woman because of the man Tom is. He has given me the space to grow. Encouraging me every step of the way, he has always supported me, in spite of my great reluctance to grow up. When we married I was paralyzingly shy. In sixteen years of school, I had never once raised my hand in class. Because of his confidence, patience, and faith in me, I've learned to overcome my shyness, often speaking before large groups and even appearing on several radio and television shows.

However, my progress didn't happen overnight. It was more like one infinitesimally small step after another, at about the same pace humans moved from walking on their knuckles to walking upright. If an exam existed for measuring patience, Tom would also be off the charts on that one.

While most people are reluctant to learn something new, Tom jumps right in. When my staging book, *This Sold House*, was ready to be published, he thought I should make more than the thirty-six cents a copy I receive as a royalty for my first book, *Spirit of the Snowpeople*. So he decided to publish it. He did a

The Lunch Bunch Regulars

great job too because we won two Midwest Book Award Gold Medals as the Best Business Book and the Best How-To Book.

Tom will tackle anything, and he won't quit until he masters it. We never hire anyone for any reason. From sheetrock work to cake decorating, from painting to wood restoration, from ceramic tile to plumbing, from roofing to deck building, Tom tackles it all. I am forever amazed and eternally grateful for everything he does for us. We've always had a lovely home, and a big part of the reason is not only the talent Tom brings to the table, but his willingness to use it.

Amazingly eclectic in his manual skills, he's even more eclectic in his vocational abilities. On the cutting edge of technology for over thirty years, Tom has worked in banking, IT, marketing, project management, website design, and real estate. And now, of course, he's also a publisher.

But his best quality, by far, is his great heart and soul-full compassion. He is a Catholic deacon and a hospital chaplain, and I know the families he serves feel blessed by his presence. Thankfully, I'm on the short list for his assistance and attention.

I would rather be with Tom than anyone else in the world; I find him endlessly fascinating, and we never run out of things to talk about even on long road trips. I could tell you more about how wonderful he is, but you'd probably close the book in disbelief. If I could clone Tom for the millions of women out there looking for a good man, I honestly would. Unfortunately for the rest of you, he's mine.

My Aunt Fran

It's difficult to write this chapter in the past tense because I started working on it one Saturday afternoon when my aunt and godmother, Fran, was still alive. I deliberately began writing her story because I thought it might keep her with us a bit longer. I was still hoping—even though she was already in the hospital and it didn't look good.

The day she told me, "I think today could be my last day," I decided it was time to write about her. I figured if Fran had anything to say about it, she might be right. She told me she'd been talking to Eileen, her long-deceased friend. "I said, Eileen, I want you to come to meet me at the pearly gates, unless you're not in heaven, in which case, forget I mentioned anything at all." Yes, that's Fran in a nutshell.

Quite simply, Fran was an original. I have no doubt Fran was *the* woman the devil was speaking of when he said, "Crap, she's awake." And I wouldn't be a bit surprised if he heard it from his Creator. Fran didn't have a "self-edit" button like the rest of us. That's the button we use to keep from saying the

The Lunch Bunch Regulars

things we're thinking, but we know are wildly inappropriate. This slight modification in her DNA made her surprising, exasperating, embarrassing, and of course, loads of fun. You just never knew what to expect.

None of us were surprised when during her last hospitalization, her doctor told us that Fran whispered in his ear, "I get the biggest kick out of getting *a rise* out of my family," which was something she did with flare, frequency, and delight.

Born January 4, 1917, she was a rebel from the get-go; a headstrong, independent, opinionated, outrageous woman, well ahead of her time. And she started young. One day she told me, "I skipped school whenever I had the chance, sassed the teachers when I thought they deserved it, and made one nun cry when I told her off for being mean to my friend." No one who knew her doubted it.

In many ways, the world, the nuns, and even her own mother, were not quite ready for Fran. She told me my grandmother asked her every day of her life, "Why can't you just be like everyone else?" But she wasn't like everyone else. In fact, she wasn't like *anyone* else.

Blessed to live to the age of ninety-three, Fran saw more living than most people, and she lived each season of her life with relish—no holds barred. But her full-out approach to life didn't keep her from having a keen sense of responsibility and duty. At the age of twenty-three, during the height of World War II, she enlisted in the U.S. Army. One day I asked her why she joined the Women's Army Corp (WACs). Then I waited for what I was sure would be some smart-aleck remark.

I got an answer I didn't expect. "I enlisted because I watched all the boys in our neighborhood go to war, and I didn't want Pa to be embarrassed because his children were all girls who weren't contributing to the war effort. I was scared to death, but it was my duty to go." As usual, she was full of surprises.

Then she simply said, "I loved my years as a mechanic in the Army." (She told me to mention she was a Tech 5.) Of course, she followed up with "Heck, it was the best way I could think of to be around so many men."

She was an amazing athlete: a speed skater, hockey player, basketball player, bowler, golfer, and baseball and softball catcher and pitcher. If you've ever seen the movie *A League of Their Own*, Fran played in a similar Midwestern semi-pro league for her employer—Montgomery Wards. She even played at Wrigley Field in Chicago. Who knows where her athletic career might have taken her if she'd had the support women's sports have today.

After her death, we found several impressive articles that

The Lunch Bunch Regulars

had been written about her in the *St. Paul Pioneer Press* newspaper during the 1940s. If you search for her name online, Frances Lanz, you'll see a picture of her in an Army Jeep, pointing at another WAC, giving her grief, no doubt.

She played softball for the WACs, and when her team needed a pitcher she stepped up and learned the skill from Gabby Street, a Major League manager at the time. As a pitcher, she led her teams to the national championship four years in a row. Still, when asked what position she played, Fran always said catcher. She saw being a pitcher as her duty, not her passion. And she always did her duty.

Years later, when my widowed grandmother called Fran unexpectedly from Minnesota to announce she'd hired a moving truck, gotten a plane ticket, and was coming to live with her in California, Fran also did her duty as a daughter. She gave up her independence and her only bedroom to care for her mother for more than seventeen years.

In her eighties, when she felt she wasn't as good a driver as she'd once been, Fran sold her car and gave up her license, again living up to what she believed was her duty as a good citizen. She said, "I've been driving since I was seven and had to strap blocks on my feet to reach the pedals, eighty years is long enough."

And when the steps at her apartment became too difficult

for her to climb, she moved into something more manageable, without fuss or fanfare. She always did what she needed to do, when she needed to do it.

Fran wasn't into stuff. We were constantly after her to buy new clothes, which she never did. San Francisco 49ers' football sweatshirts, jeans, and athletic shoes were her constant uniform. Always very generous with everyone else, she preferred taking people out to eat rather than spending money on herself. On Christmas, she gave everyone a generous check in their Christmas card, but she was a stickler about getting the cards all back so she didn't have to buy new ones, saying, "No card, no money next year."

Fran was a feminist long before the word existed. For a time, I thought she might be a lesbian because she was such a sports nut, and her preference ran to all things male. But I soon realized it was because she was so decidedly different from all the other women in my life, I couldn't find a category for her. She truly was in a class by herself.

Fran had her last date at age ninety-two, and her last proposal (an indecent one at that since it didn't include marriage) when she was ninety-one. She always said she was looking for a rich man, "with one foot in the grave and the other on a banana peel." She never found him.

The Lunch Bunch Regulars

She did marry once, but her husband expected her to come home for dinner—not fix it, just come home and eat what he'd prepared. Their marriage didn't last very long. Two years if you count the six months she needed to live in Reno to get the divorce; six weeks if you count the time they lived together.

She just was not a "married woman" kind of gal. Not long before she died, my cousins and I were going through photographs with her, and were dumbstruck by the number of handsome men we saw wrapped around our Fran. Fran told us, "I was engaged three times, maybe four, and I even broke off one engagement because he wanted several kids, and I didn't see myself living that life."

Even though she didn't want a houseful of her own kids, she loved kids and they loved her, especially the little ones. Her most recent love was our grandson, Vincent, and his little sister, Josie. On the day Vincent was born, Tom and I decided we would babysit for him one day a week. Naturally, we chose to take him every Thursday, our Wendy's lunch day. We wanted to make sure Fran could get to know her first great-great-nephew, and my mom got to spend time with her first great-grandchild.

At Vincent's very first lunch at Wendy's, when he was all of three-months old, Fran announced, "Hey there, Vincent,

I'll give you a quarter for your bank every week if you smile at me." She said she wanted him to learn the value of money. The catch, and there was always a catch with Fran, was that Vincent's smile had to be unsolicited. We couldn't coax him, or the deal was off. Well, I think Vincent understood the rule because every week when we put him in front of her, he'd flash Fran a big smile, and she'd give him a quarter.

Vincent attended a wonderful daycare where they teach the little ones sign language to help them express themselves before they can speak. The first time Vincent used the sign for "More, please" was when Fran gave him money for his bank. Our little guy learned the value of money real fast, and Fran took all the credit for it.

As he got older, and Fran became more certain of her ability to charm him, she decided it would be easier to give him one dollar a month instead. And she did. In fact, one of the last things she said to me was, "I owe Vincent and Josie each two dollars for the last two months, make sure they get it." Yes, she took her responsibilities very seriously.

The last time she was at lunch to give the kids their allowance, Vincent leaned over to me and asked, "Why is Fran's picture on the front of the dollar bill?" We all laughed like crazy, except for Fran. She was getting hard of hearing. I wish

The Lunch Bunch Regulars

I'd told her what he had said, though, because she probably would have gotten a big kick out of it. Nearly every Thursday she told us, "Vincent and Josie are my best medicine." I like to think seeing them every week kept Fran with us a while longer.

Fran was totally uninterested in women's conversation and preferred talking about football. Having lived in Northern California most of her adult life, she remained true to the San Francisco 49ers and Joe Montana after she moved back to Minnesota. But things changed when Brett Favre came to town. She did like her quarterbacks.

Without Fran, we might not have chosen Wendy's. In the interests of full disclosure, those first couple weeks we actually went to a fast-food Mexican restaurant. They had outdoor seating and the fall weather was spectacular that year. However, Fran and our Minnesota climate soon prevailed.

Fran was not a fan of Mexican food, and she flat out told us, "If you're going to eat tacos every week, I'm staying home." We also knew beautiful fall weather doesn't last very long in Minnesota, with strong north winds and piles of snow soon to follow. Fortunately for us, Wendy's was right next door.

Fran was an integral part of the reason lunching together every week worked for us. She read the newspaper cover-to-cover daily, and always had lots to say on every subject. If it

Vincent, Diane, Fran, Jolene, Jacquie,
a slice of Brian, Mom, Tom, and Sarvat.

had just been Mom and me every week, the conversation might have gotten a little stale. Fran always had something outrageous and controversial to add to keep the conversation moving. When she sensed things were slowing down, she'd wink at me and send a zinger Mom's way, which usually did the trick. Her sense of fun and spontaneity also brought other members of the family to join us at Wendy's and become part of our lunch bunch. She had a remarkable gift for drawing people to her.

After Fran died, my husband, Tom, and I were astonished to discover Fran had over one hundred and forty visits while she was in the hospital during the last ten days before her death. And those were the ones we knew about. None of them were ten-minute visits either, almost everyone stayed for hours.

At one point, her social worker called me to say we needed to do something about all of Fran's visitors. I told her, "If there's a problem you're part of it. Two members of your staff came to the hospital to visit Fran today—not for work, just for fun." And she was fun, right to the end.

Fran knew I was writing about her for this book, and during our last real visit I asked what she wanted me to say about her. She looked at me with her wide, impish grin and said, "Tell them I was a good kid." Well, Fran, you were all of that, an original, a one-of-a-kind, a good kid. Even though I don't have a single picture from our Christmas gatherings where you're not thumbing your nose at the camera, you didn't fool any of us for a minute. Your heart was as big as the sky, and we all miss you like crazy, especially me, and particularly when we're together at Wendy's.

Our First Grandchild, Vincent

By virtue of their youth, the most recent additions to the cast of regulars at our Wendy's lunches are our grandchildren, Vincent, born in October of 2007, and his little sister Josie, born in January of 2010. They have become the most impor-

My daughter Kelsey's husband John
and Vincent making silly selfies.

tant members of our clan, and given us yet another reason to gather and celebrate.

Born to our son Troy and our daughter-in-law Debbie, Vincent is our first grandchild and the first child in my family in over sixteen years. I'd never been one of those women who felt their life would be incomplete without grandchildren. Boy, I was mistaken.

Don't get me wrong, I love my children. But, for me, the older a child gets, the more I enjoy them. That is—until Vincent. Even though I'd never been a baby person, I quickly became *this baby's person*. Vincent and Josie have opened me to joy in a way I've never experienced before. Gratitude poured into every corner of my heart when each of them drew their first breath.

The Lunch Bunch Regulars

Tom and Vincent having a treat and making a memory.

Like every grandparent, I believe it's my own good fortune to have been given the two sweetest, brightest, most beautiful grandchildren on the planet. The difference, of course, is that I am right. Still, I am happy all the other grandparents have their illusions.

Grandchildren are pure delight and pure blessing. As a grandparent, I get to do everything I wish I'd taken the time to do with my own children. It is such a joy to enjoy and appreciate every nuance of their growth, revel in their sweet smiles, and wonder at each new word in their vocabulary. Every moment is a gift, every step on their journey a loving memory.

After Vincent's birth, I wrote a poem, and I'm including it here because it is an important reminder of our bond, a connection that might not have grown as strong as it is without our Wendy's lunches.

The Great Do-over

I see in your eyes, the soul of your mother.
Deep in your smile, you're so like my son.

Wholly new, and yet so familiar,
You're mine and you're not, child of my own.

I'd have missed you so much if I'd known how I'd love you,
How you'd hold my heart fast in your dear little fist.

I love you no more, but, oh, so much better
For time can't surprise me—knowing short is her bliss.

When your dad was a boy, I didn't yet grasp,
That time would steal quickly his boyness away.

Before I could stop it, he'd grown, gone and gathered
His own precious love in his arms—there to stay.

So I'll not turn my back now, you'll grow way too quickly,
I've seen it before—you'll grow faster than grass.

But I'll savor and cherish and frame every moment,
For loving you now, you're your dad in days past.

The Lunch Bunch Regulars

Loving a grandchild is like loving your child all over again without the drudgery and demands of daily life. If I'd known how wonderful grandchildren would be, I'd have had more kids. But like my brother Gary says, "Unfortunately, you knew how hard it was to raise them by the time you had two. Maybe you should have had the third one first."

On the first Thursday three-month old Vincent spent with us, Tom and I grabbed him and the diaper bag, grappled with the mysteries of car seats, and headed to lunch. While I knew I wanted Mom and Fran to get to know him, I never anticipated what his presence would mean to our little gatherings. We know now that taking our grandchildren each week was the single best decision we've ever made.

Having Vincent sitting in his car seat on the table was a little like watching television. All of us just sat and stared at him. Our conversation revolved around the question, "What did we talk about before Vincent came?" Each of us, in turn, made faces and talked with him as we held out our fingers for him to grasp in his *dear little fist.*

And we weren't alone. One member of the Wendy's staff began coming around to our table regularly to check on him. Her name is Sarvat—one of the treasures we found at Wendy's. We'd noticed her before Vincent was born. She was always polite and efficient, giving everyone her beautiful smile. But it was Vincent who gave us common ground.

The oldest of fourteen children, Sarvat helped raise every one of her brothers and sisters in her homeland of India. But instead of being burdened by these children and responsibilities, she was blessed. And she still dearly loves babies. Her own three sons now grown, Sarvat showers Vincent and Josie with her own special "baby love."

It wasn't long before we all eagerly waited for a lull in the lunch crowd so Sarvat could sneak away from the counter to visit with us. She would reach out her arms to hold Vincent, and in typical baby fashion, he'd look shy and scared, burying his face in my shoulder. Each week Sarvat would graciously say, "It's all right, Vincent, maybe next time."

We knew he had a little crush on her though, because he'd wave to her when we came, when we left, and many times in between. Soon he began toddling around the restaurant—his first stop was always to see Sarvat. And after a time, Vincent would run and jump into her arms. What a beautiful sight. On our way to Wendy's one day, the kids were playing with their toy cellphones in the car and "called" Sarvat to tell her they were running a little late on their way to see her.

The Lunch Bunch Regulars

Recently Sarvat flew to India to visit her youngest sister, age thirty-seven, who was widowed a few months ago and left with four young children. Gone for six weeks, we stopped to buy Sarvat some flowers the week she returned to work. But she beat us to the punch, greeting us at the table with beaded bracelets for Josie, special almond cakes for Vincent to take to his classmates, a wonderful hand-tiled jewelry box for Mom, and a beautiful silk shawl for me.

Vincent was not the only new face at Wendy's that year. Over the years, Tom had come to lunch with us occasionally. Now as smitten with Vincent as I was, he didn't want to miss any chances to spend time with our new grandson, so we added another place at the table. Tom's presence and help makes it possible to have conversations with the rest of the lunch bunch even if the kids aren't cooperating, "cooperating" being the operative word here.

When Vincent was two, we needed to leave Wendy's a little early one day because Vincent was, well, acting like a two-year-old. He was not pleased. As Tom struggled to buckle our unhappy, squirming bundle into his car seat, he declared, "Grandpa, I am angry. You are not cooperating with me, and your behavior is unacceptable." Later when I told Vincent he had to take a nap, he said, "I know, I know, it's non-negotiable." Can you imagine what he'll be like as a teenager? We're thankful we're just his grandparents.

My Uncle Herb

Vincent's first year with us at Wendy's brought other good changes as well. My Uncle Herb also began to come to lunch regularly. His wife, my Aunt Phyllis, died the summer before Vincent was born. Now looking for things to fill his time, Herb became a regular.

In his mid-eighties, my uncle is a wonderful man; kind, shy, self-deprecating, not at all convinced he's the great guy we all know him to be. Never one to draw attention to himself, Herb sits quietly at the opposite end of the table from Vincent. But children know things the rest of us ignore or dismiss, or are too oblivious to acknowledge. And Vincent was drawn to Herb right from the start.

As soon as he was able to walk by himself, Vincent would make his way to the other end of the table to visit Herb. After they exchanged hi-fives and fist bumps, Vincent would stand and gaze at him. Awe is the only word I can think of to describe the look on Vincent's face as he'd look at Herb. You know the look, the one a new parent reserves for their infant, the one that says, *isn't he wonderful?*

The Lunch Bunch Regulars 93

My Uncle Herb and Me.

I wonder what Vincent saw when he looked at Herb with such rapt attention. I believe the veil between the physical and the spiritual world is more transparent for the very young, and I like to think it was my Aunt Phyllis watching out for Herb, and touching his hurting heart through our grandson.

I don't notice *that* look as often anymore, now that Vincent is getting older. Sadly, it seems the veil has grown thicker. But Vincent loving Herb, and Herb taking such pleasure in him, has been a gift for all of us to witness, another miracle that wouldn't have taken place except for our weekly lunches.

Vincent and Herb still do share a special relationship. Barb, one of Herb's daughters, says her dad calls her every week to tell her what Vincent and Josie do, say, and wear. And

Herb is still one of Vincent's most important people. Whenever we have any gathering, family or otherwise, Vincent's first question is always, "Is Herb going to be there?"

When Herb joined us, the lunch bunch also got a terrific bonus—his daughter Patty. An absolute delight, my cousin is loads of fun. The laughter quotient definitely rose when she arrived. It didn't take long before Patty also became a regular, loving to watch her dad enjoying himself. And she gets such a kick out of the kids. As luck would have it, Vincent looks amazingly like Patty's son Patrick did when he was young.

Josie

Josie, baptized Josephine Lorraine (after my mother), is a beautiful, brown-eyed, dark-haired, and blissfully contented little girl. Before she was born, I thought children like Josie were a legend—mythological infants that warped, sadistic women made up to make other, less-fortunate mothers feel badly about their own colicky little darlings. Our sweet Josie Lo is the happily-ever-after child of a fairy tale.

Josie seems to take the greatest pleasure out of just being here. Unless she is hungry, sick or tired, she is happy. Not just content, she is happy, her adorable face glowing with delight at everything she sees, whether it's a raindrop on the windowpane, a set of measuring cups, or happily, me. She must know some wonderful secret to life, one I hope she never forgets. Each time I look at her, I am reminded of the quote from Charles Dickens. "What a gift it is when they who are so fresh from God, love us."

Josie couldn't wait to be born. Our daughter-in-law, Debbie, awoke the morning of January 7, 2010, with a backache and called the doctor. She was told it might be labor, but from the sound of things they had plenty of time. Fortunately, being the careful, loving parents they are, Troy and Debbie hurried off to the hospital instead.

It's a good thing they did. Although they live only ten minutes from the hospital, the worst snowstorm of the season was in full swing. For almost an hour, they sat in the midst of total freeway gridlock—the number of contractions increasing with every passing minute, and the time between them decreasing. They considered calling the police, but with cars surrounding them bumper-to-bumper, they realized it wasn't possible for the police to get to Debbie or for Troy to get her to the police.

Thankfully, we remained clueless until our nearly breathless son called with the good news. "Mom, Dad, it's a girl. She's so cute. We made it to the hospital—a whole eight minutes

Josie's first Wendy's outing.

before she was born. It was close, too close. She and Deb are doing fine, thank God, but I'm still shaking. Her name is Josie. We wanted you to be the first to know. But I've got to hang up; I've got a call to make. Josie's middle name is Lorraine—after Grandma."

Four hours later, Tom, Mom, and I sat with our sweet angel baby in our arms. She was already smiling, and she hasn't stopped yet. Neither have we. It's pretty hard not to be head over heels for a child when the first full sentence I ever heard her say was, "You are my sunshine, Grandma."

When Josie was two-years-old and discovering how to express herself, we went to the library. I suggested she go get some books so we could sit on the sofa and read together. Already an independent young lady, she came back with books for herself and a magazine for me. Plopping the magazine on my lap, she said with authority, "You read to yourself, and I'll read to myself." "Once upon a time," she would begin and slowly turn the pages. As she finished each book, she would announce for everyone to hear, "The end." Having completed her stack, she watched as I paged through the magazine she'd brought me. As I flipped through it, Josie pointed out a photo of a couple arguing, proclaiming with all the confidence of a family therapist, "That man is crabby, Grandma, he needs a Nuk (pacifier)."

It is possible Josie could also end up being a politician. When I asked her how she felt about Vincent going to all-day kindergarten, Josie tilted her head, gave it some thought and said, "Grandma, I just love missing him." On the other hand, maybe she's too honest for politics.

While Vincent is good with words, Josie excels at letters. When Tom wrote her name in caps on a picture she'd drawn she looked at it thoughtfully and said, "Grandpa, my name has a different 'e' at the end. A stickler for details, Josie's naptime is a real event. She lines up her nine stuffed animals, sometimes by size, sometimes by color, and tucks each of her "kids" in with a different blanket, kissing and hugging every one and wishing each of them "sweet dreams." It's a stall tactic, of course—but so creatively done it's impossible to be mad. This week she came out of the bedroom to say, "Grandma you need to come have a word with two of the kids. They won't listen to me." Putting on my best no-nonsense face, I gave the two "kids" a timeout and told them they had to stay in the chair till Josie got up from her nap. She looked at me and said, "I can't believe that was all it took. You can close the door on your way out Grandma, they'll be fine now. Sweet dreams."

Mom and Josie with Wendy's *Where's Waldo?* glasses.

As I write these words, I'm overwhelmed by the realization that every one of these warm memories occurred on our Wendy's lunch day. I have no words to express the gratitude I feel to have been given such happy thoughts.

My Friend Jo

No story about Wendy's would be complete without mention of my friend Jolene, whom I often call Jo, a lunch bunch regular for many years. If my mom is the most competent woman I know, Jolene is the most resourceful. She lives better than most people do, even those with a lot more money.

Divorced after twenty years of marriage, and the mother of three adult children, she owns her own home and is generous to a fault. She is the soul of moderation in all things, except travel. Jo's been to China, Peru, Turkey, Africa, Greece, England, Italy, Germany, France, Holland, Austria, Ireland, Hawaii, Alaska, and countless other places. She takes a big vacation every year and is willing to make, what I consider, huge sacrifices to do it, often eating the same meal every day for a week to save money for her trips.

She plans her purchases years in advance, knowing, to the penny, how much money she has to spend on any given day. During Lent she has gone for weeks at a time without spending a single nickel. Her motto is "Never spend more than you make, don't take more than you'll use, and don't use more than you need." She is frugal but never cheap, prudent, yet always generous.

She goes to the theater more frequently than most ardent

patrons, often working as an usher to get a complimentary ticket. She makes the most of every coupon. She knows where all the best deals in town are, and if there's a free event anywhere, Jo is there.

In all honesty, I must admit without her perseverance we would not have become friends. Jolene and I met about thirty years ago through a small faith community at our church. At the time, I was very involved with my kids, my job, and my volunteer work, and I was not looking for a new friend.

Jo's persistence, her quiet manner, and her singular way of looking at the world won me over. Jolene is a truly unique individual. She is, as our mutual friend Patrick says, "A voice of wisdom in the world." I know she has been, and continues to be, a voice of wisdom in my world. I can always count on her to broaden my mind with the view rarely held.

I remember the moment I first realized what a treasure she was. We were having a discussion with our church group about living on a limited income. Granted, no one I know could speak as expertly on this topic as Jolene, but her answer still continues to inspire me all these years later. Rarely does a week go by when I'm not reminded of it.

When I asked her how she reconciled working at a high-end department store like Marshall-Fields without having the money to shop there, without hesitation, she replied, "Oh, I own it all, I just let other people dust it."

She embodies a spirit of largesse that is positively magnetic to be around. Although I know her well, I am constantly surprised at her take on things, and can seldom predict the path her mind will follow. Her particular way of looking at life creates a sense of possibility that often stretches me further than I want to go. But I always appreciate the trip, even if it takes me a while to arrive.

Recently, we were driving down a divided highway where our community had just added trees and grass to the median. In my oh-so-common way, I began complaining about all the money it was going to take for the upkeep of the unnecessary landscaping. Without hesitation, Jolene said, "Yes, isn't it great? Think about all the people who will have jobs caring for the grass, and how happy they are." What can I say; she's one in a million.

Our lunch bunch would not be the same without Jolene, and neither would our family. For many years now, Jolene has not only been part of our Wendy's experience, but also a cherished member of our family who attends all our family gatherings and holiday celebrations.

After Vincent's last birthday party, I noticed him sitting

alone in a corner. When I asked him what was wrong. He said, "It was my worst birthday ever. My cousin had to leave early and Jolene couldn't come because she's in California." Where did the family bonding begin? Where else, at Wendy's.

She adds an element of surprise, with her uncommon opinions on life, and spontaneity with her frequent and unexpected gifts. It might be freshly baked cookies, newly minted coins, bags of potatoes, or the slant on party politics you never considered. With Jo you never know, and therein lay the charm.

Spend time with those you love. One of these days you will say either, "I wish I had or I'm glad I did."—Unknown

Chapter Seven

A Golden Thread

There's something like a line of gold thread running through a man's words when he talks to his daughter, and gradually over the years it gets to be long enough…to weave into a cloth that feels like love itself.—John Gregory Brown

Like me, my dad had his youth stolen from him. World War II took his young life; not the breath from his body, but the light of innocence from his eyes. It took me many years to understand how much his experience affected our family.

Unfailingly kind, a good provider, a loving father, and a devoted husband, Dad loved my mother and his family very much. But memories of the war followed him most of his life. Every day he went to work, came home and napped till supper, then lay on the floor and watched TV till the wee hours of the morning when he would finally go to bed. I wonder now if he thought staying up until he was exhausted would keep him from having bad dreams about the war.

My parents came from a time and culture that believed it was better not to look back, but to march on. And so we didn't know much about Dad's war experiences. We knew he'd been on Normandy Beach and at the Battle of the Bulge. And we also knew at some point, he and his buddy took a Jeep and went to Paris. Shortly after they arrived, my dad left the hotel to get cigarettes. When he returned, he found his friend dead from a self-inflicted gunshot wound.

Like a lot of veterans, my dad didn't talk about the war, but I don't think it kept him from thinking about what happened. Only after I was married, did I realize my dad's recurring nightmares were not because he was dreaming of having a car accident, like my mother told us, but more likely, because of nightly visits by grisly phantoms of Normandy Beach and the gruesome scenes of his other war memories.

Only once do I recall Dad speaking about the horror of his wartime experience. A family friend had just returned from a business conference in Washington, D.C. It was shortly after the opening of the city's Holocaust museum. When she

A Golden Thread

spoke about her powerful visit with great feeling, my dad quietly said, "I could never go there." She continued, saying how important it is for younger generations to know the horror of what happened. Again my dad said, "I could never go there." Finally my dad rose from his chair and quietly left the room, saying under his breath, "I was at Auschwitz the day after liberation, I can still smell it."

It doesn't take a lot of imagination to fill in the blanks. My dad, like so many young soldiers both then and now, are haunted by visions of things no one should ever have to see, much less experience. Unfortunately for them, the lesson too many of us learn as children is still the same: *Soldier up, don't look back, and march on.*

Recently I was saddened to discover soldiers today suffering from post-traumatic stress are still shamed into silence by their 'braver' comrades, just as they were in wars past. And, today many of them still commit suicide like my dad's friend, rather than live with the pain of their experience. We inflict suffering and we suffer, we kill and we die, still we learn nothing.

My dad's war experience turned him into a pacifist. He always said, "If you're going to bomb someone, bomb them with food and clothing. Making your enemies love you is a lot more effective way to end a war than creating more enemies." I agree with Dad.

Dad wasn't part of our weekly lunch bunch at the beginning, but he was part of the ritual. Every week, I would go to my parents' house before we went to lunch. I'd find my dad sitting in his favorite chair, in the corner of the living room next to the fireplace, and we'd chat.

Mom would be putting the finishing touches on Fran's hair, and Dad and I would talk until they were ready to go to lunch. One week while we waited I showed him the manuscript for my children's book. He encouraged me to write more and find a publisher. I've always been grateful to know I had his support for my writing.

Mostly though, our conversations were about the weather, the latest golf tournament, Dad's garden—nothing very deep or provocative, just ordinary chats. Until then, any opportunity to talk with Dad had almost always included Mom. Now, because Mom was tied up doing Fran's hair, this became our special time together. When we left for lunch, the three of us would often ask Dad if he wanted to come to Wendy's. For the first year and a half, he politely declined. When we'd return from lunch, we'd find him right where we left him, still sitting in his favorite chair.

A Golden Thread

Then June 6, 1996 arrived—the 52nd anniversary of D-Day. As I sat watching the repeat of a special hosted by Peter Jennings about Normandy Beach, I cried thinking of what my dad had experienced. For the first time, I truly realized how young he'd been, only 20 years old, younger than my own son, Troy, when he'd seen such violence, destruction, and human devastation.

The film footage was horrifying to watch. It was hard to believe it was real, and even harder to comprehend the human (and I use the word 'human' loosely) capacity for cruelty. The screen was filled with random bodies and body parts floating in an ocean red with the blood of innocents. I couldn't imagine, and didn't want to think about, my dad being there and being expected to continue fighting while witnessing such a massacre.

I remembered how Dad had reacted on the eve of the first Gulf War, when talk of reinstating the draft began. On the day American bombs first fell on Kuwait, January 16, 1991, Troy turned nineteen and became eligible for the draft. With tears in his eyes, Dad had said, "I will not let Troy go to war. I'll take him to Canada, or go somewhere they'll never find him." Dad was ready to do anything to keep his grandson from going to Iraq. After I saw the film of Normandy Beach, I understood why.

When the program ended I wanted desperately to call him, but I was scared. I'd grown up with the no-talk rule, the taboo about any mention of World War II. I knew I would be violating a sacred boundary, still I felt compelled to break the silence.

My dad never answered the phone unless Mom was gone, but I knew she was with her bridge group that evening. With tears in my eyes, I grabbed the phone, and without a single thought in my head about what I was going to say, I dialed, sending a prayer to the heavens for guidance. When Dad answered I said, "Dad, I know you don't ever talk about the war, but I was just watching a special about Normandy Beach, and I am sorry for all you went through to keep the world safe for us."

My dad said "Okay," and hung up.

The next week I went over for our pre-Wendy's ritual as usual. I remember it so clearly. Dad and I were outside talking about lawn care, another of our usual topics. Mom popped her head out the door and asked, "Gordie, are you sure you don't want to come with us to Wendy's today?"

To my great surprise, Dad said, "Yes, I think I'll come."

Mom and Fran always drove together, and I drove alone. As Mom and Fran got in the car, Dad said the sweetest words I'd ever heard from him, "I'll ride with Diane." And he did. Week after week, every time we would get in the car I would hear him say, "I'll ride with Diane."

Each time I heard those magic words, my heart would

sing. Dad chose ME. The first time he said it I had all I could do not to burst into tears. I held it together on the ride to Wendy's and during our lunch. I held it together when I dropped him off at home. But the moment he was out of the car, I began to weep. I cried so hard I had to pull over and stop at Target for a box of tissues. And by the time I finally stopped crying later that afternoon, something had changed in me—something had broken open. The big chip I had carried around on my shoulder for so long had fallen off and floated away on tears of joy.

He never mentioned the phone call I made to him on the anniversary of D-Day. But I will always believe my small gesture made all the difference, creating a bond between us that kept him coming to lunch every week. You wouldn't think a mile and a half trip to a fast-food restaurant could be that important. But it was. Our conversation was the same as it had been sitting in the living room, but it was exclusive, it was private, and it was *ours*. Best of all, after nearly 50 years there was an *us*.

It feels almost unbearably special to be chosen, especially if, like me, you've ever experienced the pain of not being chosen for the team, or a big promotion, or an invitation to the big dance.

Dad's choosing me each week was a benediction, a blessing

that continued until our last lunch together, July 15, 1999, and will bless me forever. The memory of this particular day is still crystal clear in my mind all these years later. I don't remember the words, but I know how they felt. You know the feeling you get when you're incredibly happy—and yet laughter isn't exactly the right response. You smile so big you know you look like an idiot, and you don't even care. A fountain of happiness bubbles up inside, and you know if you say too much, or laugh too loud, the best part of the magic will float away and escape with the bubbles. Well, I feel all those things when I think of our last lunch together.

How the topic came up, I'm not sure, but Mom and Dad started talking about their courtship. Dad was sitting with his arm around Mom in the Wendy's booth, looking more like teenagers in love than a couple who'd recently celebrated fifty-five years of marriage. With pride in his voice and a twinkle in his eye, he said, "You know, Diane, your mother was a terrible flirt. I was only one among many who wanted her more than she wanted me." Mom was mortified, of course, and vehemently disagreed, all the while blushing like the sweet young girl she once was.

I'm not sure whom to believe, even today. Mom was a knockout and Dad looked like Elvis—my friends told me so.

He had an absolutely killer smile, the same smile he still wore for my mom at Wendy's during our last lunch.

After lunch Mom mentioned she was going to stop at Penney's to shop for a new pair of shoes. Not much of a shopper himself, Dad reached into his pocket and handed her some money, "Lorraine, why don't you pick up a new skirt, too."

Mom gave him a quizzical look. "I don't need a new skirt."

My dad smiled shyly and quipped, "Oh, but I do. I want to see more of your legs."

"Oh, Gordie," Mom fussed as she rolled her eyes. But I saw her reach over and squeeze his hand under the table.

Have you ever felt like you're not actually participating in an event, like some part of you is completely separate and watching the action from somewhere outside yourself? If you have, you know how I felt as I watched them—like a fly on the wall, eavesdropping on a beautiful love scene. Sometimes you can have a wonderful experience, but it's only in retrospect you realize how special it was. On that wonderful day I was given a great gift, the grace to recognize the miracle sitting right in front of me. I remember feeling absolutely giddy to have parents who were still so much in love. I knew I would hold the joy of this day in my heart forever. And I have.

On his way to play a round of golf with friends, we said

good-bye in the doorway at Wendy's instead of at home. We embraced, as we always did now. And as he hugged me, I whispered in his ear what he whispered in mine. "I love you." I didn't know this would be our final good-bye—but it was, and it's a gift of love I'll always treasure.

Two days later, Dad was gone. He died of an aneurysm while Mom was out buying him blueberries. As I held his hand in the ER, and my family prepared to take Dad off life support, my mind dwelt on two things. I was grateful Dad would no longer have to think dark thoughts about Normandy Beach, Battle of the Bulge, Auschwitz, and all the other pieces of hell he'd seen. And I thanked God for Wendy's and every lunch we shared together—especially the last one.

Sometimes you will not know the value of a moment, until it becomes a memory.—Dr. Suess

Chapter Eight

A Happy Accident

Don't fix it if it ain't broke.—Bert Lance

Over the years, people have asked why we don't spread our wings and try other restaurants. It's not likely to happen.

In the beginning, Wendy's was a happy accident—a matter of convenience. But before long, we saw the serendipity in our choice. Where else would we go where we could seat four or fourteen, depending on who shows up?

Each week we start our lunch with three tables pushed together, but as time passes and family and friends arrive, we sometimes have as many as seven or eight tables lined up. It's a wonderful sight. Nothing makes me happier than needing to add another table.

And, of course, if you want people to come, it helps to make it financially accessible for everyone. Sometimes several members of one family show up, and it's nice to know it's not creating a money crunch for them or for any of the hardworking college students in the family. After all, unlike Vincent and Josie, not everyone has a patron like Fran.

The staff in Roseville is like family to us, and we know they feel the same. I told you about Sarvat, but I haven't told you about Jacque, who is very special to all of us. She was the manager of the Roseville Wendy's location, for sixteen of the twenty-two years we've lunched there.

A grandma to her own three little ones, Jacque has always paid special attention to our family. Nothing escaped her notice. For instance, a month before Fran's death, Mom and Fran arrived early for lunch one day and decided to sit in the car and chat till more of us arrived. Jacque knew Fran's health had begun to fail and, ever vigilant, she went out to the car to check on them to make sure they were all right. When Fran died, Jacque asked Wendy's to send a memorial to Fran's favorite charity, which meant a lot to our family.

Over the years, we've had hundreds of wonderful times at Wendy's. Sometimes lunch lasts an hour, and sometimes it

A Happy Accident

goes on for two and a half hours. We've planned holiday menus, vacations, and weddings, and other times, we've grieved. However, in all these years, never has a week gone by when I haven't been glad we came.

During the summer when school is out, our group is usually larger. My sister Gail is one of our summer lunchers. A pied piper with children, she is a favorite of Vincent and Josie, and is always ready to play with them and let them listen to her recordings of Raffi and Bob Dylan, two of Vincent's favorites. What can I say? He has eclectic tastes.

Josie's no slouch in the music department either. On our way to Wendy's one day, I asked her if she'd like to listen to the Itsy, Bitsy Spider CD. "No, Grandma," she said seriously. "I'm in the mood for *Move It Like Jagger*. And play it LOUD, I like it when it tickles my eardrums." I guess a lot has changed since I was young.

To Mom's delight, my brothers, Gary and Brian also come once in a while if they can sneak away from work for a quick lunch. Gail's son, Steve, my godson, who's working on his master's degree and is a soccer coach at the University of Wisconsin–River Falls, comes nearly every week, finding the time in his busy schedule to drive the one hundred mile round trip to join us. He told me once he considers Vincent his nemesis, threatening to replace him in my affections, but it's never going to happen because we've been buddies forever.

Our kids, Kelsey and Troy, adults now themselves, don't get to join us often, but we celebrate when they do. After college, Kelsey worked on archeological digs from the Grand Canyon to Belize, and managed the Paleontology lab at the Science Museum of Minnesota, working as a conservation archeologist there. Unfortunately, several years ago she was rear-ended by a drunk driver in a life-changing accident that forced her to give up her work and embark on a new career. But, like her grandmother, Kelsey excels at making lemonade out of lemons. Kelsey now lives in a small town in Michigan while her husband John works on his Ph.D. She is making a living as an artist, something we are very proud of since most artists are unable to support themselves with their art, even in big cities.

When Kelsey brought her "friend" John, home to meet us, Tom and I knew he was "the one." It wasn't hard for us to figure out—how many couples both love dinosaurs, Legos, and rocks? It was a match made in heaven—or Legoland. Nevertheless, it took nearly ten years of friendship before the timing was right, and as Kelsey says, "The curtain rose on John." He is smart, funny, competent, an outstanding teacher, and unlike most academic types, he is extremely handy. Besides, he loves our girl. What else is there?

Kelsey misses living in the Twin Cities near all of us, and we miss her too. She and John always arrange their visits home so they include Thursday at Wendy's. Catching up with the whole gang at once makes even the shortest trip home worthwhile. She told me recently that Thursdays are the hardest day of the week for her, saying, "I seem to miss you and Dad most when I know you're all together at lunch—spending time I can never get back." I know it's true. To keep Kelsey in the loop, I call her each week after our lunch to relate the latest family news and stories. Although she claims to love hearing them, she often cries.

Occasionally, our son, Troy, or his wife, Debbie, may drop in to give Vincent and Josie a quick kiss when they are out of school, but their days are very busy, so it doesn't happen often. Troy is a master craftsman in the truest sense of the word. We let him remodel our home when he was eighteen, which included some demolition and an addition, and gives you an idea of how good he is at what he does. It wasn't much of a risk though—we knew by then he had a gift.

When he was two and a half, he'd removed all the heat vents and cold air returns in the house, unscrewed the entire back deck of our hatchback car, and opened a gallon of pink paint, and painted an entire window frame with a sash tool—without getting a single drop on the screen itself. Like his father, there's not much our boy can't do.

Troy and a friend own an environmentally friendly countertop company, and have developed a process to make completely "green" countertops. Beautiful as well as virtually indestructible, they're made from recycled glass, walnut shells, and any number of unexpected ingredients—bringing recycling to a whole new level. Troy has even perfected a process using coal slag. It is gorgeous. Its blue-black iridescence, complemented by the polished surface, creates a stunning combination. Their company is getting a lot of positive press these days. Their countertops are in the new Atlanta Braves stadium, and we're certain that his long hours, talent, and hard work will pay off soon.

Like Kelsey and John, Debbie and Troy knew each other for ten years before they began dating. Interested in Deb long before he dated her, Troy was reluctant to put their wonderful friendship at risk. We are glad he did. She is everything we could have asked for in a daughter-in-law and more: a wonderful wife and loving mother; terrific cook, homemaker, designer and high-performance businesswoman, and she is fun, fun, fun.

A Happy Accident

Both of our children have married very well. If we had handpicked life partners for our children, we could not have done better. Tom and I love both John and Debbie, and feel blessed to have them in our family.

Gail's daughter, my niece Ashley, and her husband Maxwell, recently moved back to Minnesota after two years in Texas and Alabama where Maxwell flew personnel and supplies out to oil rigs, and trained helicopter pilots for the U.S. Army. On several occasions during their time away they managed to get a few days off and made quick trips home, often managing to attend our Thursday get-togethers. During one short layover, Maxwell arranged with my nephew Steve (Ashley's brother) to surprise us by bringing him to lunch. What a treat! All of us agreed we learned more about him that day than we had in all our family gatherings. We would never have seen him during that short stopover without the Wendy's connection. None of us can explain or understand it, but we know something special happens at lunch.

The week they moved back home, we found Ashley and Maxwell waiting at the table for us when we arrived. Thrilled to see them, we were chattering like crazy about their plans. Maxwell had applied for his dream job, flying emergency helicopters for the Mayo Clinic in Rochester. Just as he was telling us about it, his phone rang. He looked at the number, and whispered, "It's Mayo." We held our breath while he took the call. But the look on his face told us what we wanted to know. He got the job. Another Thursday, and another celebration—courtesy of the hospitality that has brought us together every week for more than twenty years.

If we're lucky we might get a brief glimpse of Andrew or Carly, our more cosmopolitan twenty-something niece and nephew. Carly moved to Chicago about a few years ago, and though we all encouraged her sense of adventure, we hoped it would be temporary. Although the lure of Chi-town was strong, she met a wonderful man and fortunately for all of us, Nate is also from the Twin Cities, which doubled the odds of her return. And they did—just in time for their wedding in June.

The cast of characters changes every year, with more of the kids having their own transportation, and others moving on to college, and/or full-time jobs. New friends, fiancés, and spouses are always joining the family and the lunch bunch. One month last fall we had visitors from Texas, Alabama, Michigan, Colorado, and Illinois. Lunch at Wendy's is a lot like weather in Minnesota, things change quickly, but each season has its own charm.

A Happy Accident

People are always asking me to tell more stories about the Wendy's lunches. After all, you'd think I would have collected hundreds of them by now. But the truth is that most of what happens at Wendy's doesn't really translate into stories. Every lunch is made up of a hundred little sound bites and even more subtle glances. Like when Josie was little and Vincent handed her a french fry and she said, "Tank you, Binsen," and we all smiled at each other.

Or when Vincent went through his pipe phase, and he sat at lunch each week for a month with a miniature corncob (bubble) pipe hanging out of the corner of his mouth, and using it to gesture, ala Hemingway. The comments and conversations, while they may not be significant or even funny in

Celebrating my cousins' visit from Texas.

themselves, seem to take on the glow of the entire twenty-two-year experience. Maybe you just have to be there.

However, one story has remained a favorite. When the cousins were all small, I would pick up Derek and Lee, my brother Brian and his wife Laura's boys, every week in the summer so they could join us. One memorable lunch conversation was about who knew their right hand from their left. When it was time for seven-year-old Lee to answer, he told us proudly, "Of course, I know my right hand from my left." He paused and then added, "Unless I turn around." I laughed the hardest—because being a lefty myself, I know exactly what he meant. I still have trouble with the right and left thing. If I ever lose my wedding ring, I'm in real trouble.

In his book, *The Seven Habits of Highly Effective People*, Stephen Covey talks about building emotional bank accounts, creating trust, and fostering relationships with kindness, communication, and respect. When I read his book, I knew that dynamic is precisely what is present when we come together for lunch each week. With every kindness and courtesy, and by our mutual dedication to be there, all of us are making deposits in each other's emotional bank accounts. The power of showing up cannot be

A Happy Accident

We expected six people, but nine more
showed up including two of my Mom's
grandchildren and four great-grandchildren.

underestimated—more powerful than words, is our commitment to be together—disregarding the 'no-talk' rule.

Those long lazy summer days when our own kids and our nieces and nephews were young were wonderful. Tom and I owned house with a pool at the time, so we often made a day of it, with everyone coming back to our house for a swim after lunch. On those Thursdays, our Wendy's lunches sometimes lasted well into the evening, with the rest of the family coming to join the lunch bunch for dinner.

One week stands out in my mind as a time when the value of our weekly lunches came home to me. It was the week my dad died. He died on a Saturday evening in July, and on Sunday the entire family came over to swim. Each day during that long hot week, we gathered to do what needed to be done, to swim, and share our memories of Dad. I've always thought our weekly lunches gave us a comfort level being together that sustained us and brought us consolation during those difficult days.

The day after Dad's funeral, sixteen of us gathered for lunch at Wendy's. Mom, Fran, my siblings and kids, nieces, nephews, cousins, and friends, all came to plan a vacation together for the following month at Lutsen, a resort on Lake Superior, not far from the Canadian border. As I looked around the table, I knew I was witnessing the sustaining power of family and community—proof that life does go on. And I sent a silent prayer of thanks for the many unexpected gifts my family has found there.

He is a wise man who does not grieve for the things which he has not, but rejoices for those which he has.—Epictetus

Chapter Nine

Where's the Beef?

Courtesies of a small and trivial character are the ones which strike deepest in the grateful and appreciating heart.
—Henry Clay

What has made lunch at Wendy's so life changing for me?

It seems obvious now that gratitude was the game changer. It's hard to understand how it escaped me for so long. Tom and I have known for years the reason we are happily married is, at least in part, because we are grateful for our relationship. Almost every day we say to each other, "We are blessed to have such a wonderful marriage, and to be so happy together." And our saying it has made it so. Somehow we understood from the beginning, our words had the power to create our reality—the gratitude we feel for finding a life together calls the nature of our relationship into being.

Recently I discovered a declaration is "a statement of intention in the absence of any actual evidence." The framers of the Declaration of Independence, with no government in place, called our country into being with their beautiful words, "We hold these words to be self-evident." Engaged couples declare their love and speak their marriage into reality. When we claim something to be so, it becomes so. This is why we say "Amen," which means "and so it is," at the end of a prayer.

The more we dwell on gratitude, the more reasons to feel grateful show up in our lives. As soon as I quit dwelling on my unhappy past and allowed myself to feel gratitude for a simple and successful lunch with Mom, the course of my life began to change.

In his book, *The Hidden Messages In Water,* Dr. Masaru Emoto proved in his amazing photographs, an expression of love or gratitude said over water crystals transforms them into beautiful crystalline structures. Correspondingly, if negative, destructive words are used, the crystal forms become ugly and distorted. If you consider the human body is largely water, it is not surprising our words of love or hate can create a powerful transformation in ourselves, and in others. It's no wonder gratitude is so powerful.

When I went to my parents' house that Thursday morning more than twenty years ago, I knew my destructive thoughts were ruining my life, but I didn't yet understand I was the one responsible for thinking them. They weren't imposed upon me like my eye color; I was choosing them again and again, but they were not serving me.

Albert Einstein said, "Insanity is doing the same thing over and over and expecting different results."

I needed to commit to do things differently if I wanted a different outcome.

Until I made a new choice, I didn't realize I had an alternative available to me. I needed to think new thoughts, to let go of my sad story, before I could become aware of other possibilities. Realizing I had another option opened me to grace and life in a way completely unknown to me.

One of my heroes, Mother Teresa said, "Very little in life comes to you without saying yes." My dream of finding a better, more joyful way to be in the world began with a yes. And because my mom also said yes, we started the ball rolling, a decision which has enriched so many lives. Our commitment to each other has kept the home fires burning ever brighter for more than two decades now.

Tom and I have been through a number of personal challenges in the intervening years, difficulties we never expected to face. Our family and our faith have been tested, and they have proved our solace. Many times in the last several years, our weekly lunch at Wendy's has been one of the few bright spots during some very dark days.

> **What a gift it is, when something as simple, affordable, and fun as eating with family, can continually recharge your batteries and give you the courage to fight the good fight.**

For too much of my life, I was the kind of person who woke up in the morning and said, "Crap, I'm still here." I am so grateful I'm no longer that woman. With all the trials we've faced, I don't even like to consider what I'd be like today had I not been graced with a little insight and a dollop of ketchup.

Happiness is not something ready-made. It comes from your own actions.—The Dalai Lama

Chapter Ten

Returning to the Table

In every conceivable manner, the family is our link to our past, the bridge to our future. —Alex Haley

As a country, we need to start eating together again. Countless people ask me why having lunch together one day a week has been so valuable to our family. However, until I did some research, I had no specific answers. Oh, I knew it was in spending time together, but although I sensed there was more to it, I never would have guessed how much more. In my investigation, I've found few things pay as many dividends, with less effort and more enjoyment, than sharing a meal.

Eating together connects us in ways most people would never consider, but are undeniable once you spend some time thinking about them. Children indirectly learn many things at the family table. Because they are sitting in on adult conversations, something they would probably never choose to do on their own, they hear new ideas along with more adult conversation. This helps them increase their vocabularies and their capacity for creative thought. And the best part is that this process happens effortlessly, by osmosis, not with long hours of study.

Perhaps being exposed to adult conversation could explain what Vincent said to me when I suggested we read *Curious George,* "Grandma, I believe you misspoke, you do not have *Curious George* at your house; the book is at our house." Many people go through their entire lives without using the word "misspoke." I guess they haven't been fortunate enough to dine with Vincent. He was right, we'd read it at his house, not ours.

And since a larger vocabulary is key to improved literacy, and because literacy is a good predictor of success in school, it's clear eating together bodes well for the future of our children. Maybe instead of "No Child Left Behind," it should be "No Child Eats Alone."

Tom and I also think our lunches at Wendy's have increased our grandchildren's attention span and their ability to enjoy adult company. Recently we took them out to lunch with a friend of ours and noticed both of them were easily able to spend the entire lunch chatting with us—behaving just as maturely as the rest of us—although that is not always a ringing endorsement.

Children also learn manners at the dinner table. No one over fifty will argue with the fact that kids' table manners have deteriorated significantly in the last thirty years. My own theory blames the advent of the microwave for hastening the demise of the family meal, and clearing the way for the whole "eating-on-the-run" mentality to take its place.

Laura Barclay, international etiquette authority and founder of the Civility & Etiquette Centre, says, "If you expect young people to learn proper table manners for dining at home and in restaurants, they need practical experience. Learning how to make appropriate dinner conversation, how to build their knowledge and confidence in conversations with adults and each other, are skills built around having regular family meals together. Not doing so can put a child at a disadvantage throughout their lives, whether it's finding a life partner, applying for college, or interviewing for a new job."

In addition, Ms. Barclay states that dining as a family "can effortlessly help children learn the guidelines of dining etiquette so that they can instead focus on the conversations and time together, which is at the heart of meal time together, whether they are with family, friends, or future employers."

The ability to cook a meal in a few minutes took the necessity of a daily dinner hour out of family schedules. Before microwaves, families ate together because it was too inconvenient to do anything else. However, everything changed when Johnny could heat up his own meal whenever he chose, and didn't need to be home for dinner with his family. And because Johnny didn't come home, neither did his sister. Finally, it wasn't even worth it for Mom or Dad to cook a family meal because no one was at home to eat it. It becomes difficult to develop table manners if you never sit at the table.

And it's a slippery slope. As table manners have dwindled, so too have many other courtesies. I googled cell phone etiquette and found myriad articles condemning the lack of phone courtesy in cell phone users—not to mention using cell phones at the dining table. Anyone with Internet access has seen first-hand the inappropriate content on Facebook, LinkedIn, Twitter, and email postings.

Don't even get me started on texting. An acquaintance told me recently her daughter had a pajama party, and when she looked in the family room to see why the girls were so quiet, she discovered they were all texting instead of talking. Such stories speak volumes, in an altogether disturbing way, about the future of relationships and our ability to communicate with each other.

Miriam Weinstein, author of *The Surprising Power of Family Meals,* says, "Sitting down to a meal together draws a line around us. It encloses us and…strengthens the bonds that connect us with other members of our self-defined clan." In other words, dining together gives us a sense of belonging and personal worth—boundaries to teach us what is appropriate and what is not, what is required, tolerated, and what is forbidden. It imbues us with the accepted social mores of our clan and our world. And, if the current state of things is any indicator, it must be true because many children seem to have fewer boundaries than ever before.

Research shows if a family regularly eats together, the children are happier, healthier, and become better students. It also reveals kids who eat with their families more often have higher self-esteem, less depression, fewer suicidal thoughts, and use less alcohol and fewer drugs. It makes sense that the psychological stress and isolation associated with the teenage years would be diminished by being regularly surrounded with those who love them most, and who give them support and encouragement.

Such information comes to us through the impartial lens of research. However, one benefit stands out which any adult is able to personally confirm. *Family history is passed on at meals.* At the table, we find out who we are, what we stand for, and where we come from. The conversation may move from the dining table to the sofa, but it almost always starts between the mashed potatoes and the blueberry pie or, in this case, between a baked potato and a Frosty. Quite literally, the table defines us as family—immediate, extended, adopted, or singularly unique—it gives us our identity and encourages us to claim it. It lets us know our presence is valued, and we are loved. Could anything be more important than that?

Eating without conversation is only stoking.—Anonymous

Chapter Eleven

It *Is* a Wonderful Life

This is what I wished for.
—Mary Bailey in *It's a Wonderful Life*

I can't help but think of the great Christmas movie classic, *It's a Wonderful Life,* when I consider what life might have been without our family lunches.

In the movie, Jimmy Stewart plays George Bailey, a kind and decent man who spends his life making things better for the people in his hometown. Through no fault of his own, he ends up responsible for $8,000 missing from his Bedford Falls Savings and Loan business, and realizes he might be sent to jail. Drunk and suicidal, he tries to kill himself, but is rescued by Clarence, an angel who shows George what life would be like for his loved ones had he never been born. In the end, George realizes he has touched many people, and discovers he really does have a wonderful life.

George and I have a lot in common. It may have been Clarence, the apprentice angel, who helped George find his wings, but it was Wendy's that helped me find mine. Undoubtedly, life would have gone on if we had never started having lunch at Wendy's. But things would have been very different.

Would I have resolved my childhood issues with my family? I'd like to think so, but it doesn't seem likely. I was pretty stuck. Even though I can imagine growing up enough to let go of my old baggage, somehow I doubt Mom and I would have the very special relationship we have today if it hadn't been for the commitment we made to have lunch together each week.

Mom and I talk on the phone every evening, like we have ever since the day Dad died. Once in a while, life throws us a curve ball and we aren't able to have our talk-time together, but not very often. And when we can't connect for our nightly chat, something important is absent from my life, and I feel like I'm going to bed without being *tucked in*. If lunch hadn't opened the door for us, I'd have missed thousands of conversations, even more laughs, and countless per-

It Is *a Wonderful Life*

sonal moments I'll treasure forever. I have so many reasons to feel grateful.

Would I have established my unique relationship with my dad, or told him I was sorry he'd had to fight in the war? I doubt it. I tend to think the status quo would have prevailed. Not much time was left because Dad died about three years after he began coming to lunch with us. The emotional bank account I built with him during our weekly visits when Mom, Fran and I first began going to lunch, gave me the courage to call Dad on the anniversary of D-Day. It was that call that changed everything between us. Those early visits with Dad, while I waited for Mom and Fran, provided the cushion, letting me know if the conversation didn't go well, the emotional bank account was still brimming with plenty of deposits.

Would Tom and I have gotten to know Vincent and Josie the way we have without our lunches? Would they have gotten to know us? I hope so but I'm not sure. Because Troy and Debbie both work long hours all week and like to stay home with the kids on weekends, it seems unlikely we would have been able to spend as much time with our grandchildren as we do now.

I'm certain we wouldn't initially have made the choice to take Vincent one day a week without Wendy's, because even with Wendy's, it was a big decision. Tom and I are both still working and very happy to be empty nesters. Being ignorant of the bliss of grandparenting, we were reluctant to surrender our freedom. And although it's hard for me to imagine now, we would not have missed what we didn't know.

Taking baby Vincent on our lunch day was a powerful motivator for us because it meant Mom and Fran would get to see him every week. Planning to spend part of each Thursday at lunch with Vincent meant we would not only be sharing him with our family, but also sharing some of the responsibility. It meant more arms to hold him and more hearts to love him. Somehow knowing we would have their help made the challenge more manageable, and the choice easier. Without a doubt, our weekly lunch at Wendy's was the driving force in our decision to care for our grandchildren one day a week. Vincent's birth created a new opportunity for us and for our family. It was another reason to love each other and to spend time together, one I wouldn't even have considered, much less understood, in years past. We had no idea how such a decision would enrich our lives and change us. Life is better, I am happier, with Vincent, Josie, and Wendy's in my life.

It's awe-inspiring to look down the table and see four generations gathered. Very simply, I discovered the value of family at Wendy's. You may think I'm exaggerating, but I'm not. Be-

It Is *a Wonderful Life*

Together again.

fore Wendy's, time spent with my family often had *obligation* attached to it. After Wendy's, family time became an opportunity—a gift. It became, and still remains sacred.

And the ripples on our family waters continue to swell. An inclusive group, we're always open to anyone who wishes to join us. Recently, as my cousin Patty waited to order, she overheard someone behind her in line say, "I don't know what's going on with that group. Every time I come here more people are sitting at their table." The same day, a high school friend of Patty's saw us and asked if he could join us for lunch the next time he's in the area. We hope he does. Bigger is better. That's what's going on with our group.

And Herb, well, without our lunch group, Uncle Herb would

have been a guy Vincent saw a couple times a year at big family gatherings, whose name he probably would not have even known. Instead, Herb is the patriarch in Vincent and Josie's life, their honorary great-grandfather; someone with whom they share the cherry tomatoes from their salads, and bake cupcakes for, someone they love, look up to, and will remember forever.

A while ago when we were leaving Wendy's, Vincent walked Herb to the door and hugged him good-bye. The instant he left, Vincent ran back, tugged on my arm and begged, "Will you take me to Herb's car so I can kiss him good-bye. Hurry! I love him. Herb is one of the greatest men in the whole wide world." We did. And when I told Herb what Vincent said, with tears in his eyes and a tremor in his voice, he said, "That's very high praise coming from you, Vincent." I cried all the way home, overwhelmed by the blessings that flow our way, asking nothing of us but to show up and eat lunch together one day a week.

And our Wendy's family continues to grow. My brother Gary and my sister-in-law Katie, are new grandparents, thanks to their son Paul and his wife Casey. And good news for the Wendy's lunch bunch—Casey will be staying home with the baby for a while. With any luck, they'll be our newest lunch bunch regulars.

It Is a Wonderful Life

The lunch bunch—eight tables for fifteen of us.

Some time ago, Troy, Debbie, Vincent and Josie came over for supper, along with Mom and my grade school friend Nancy. Vincent and Nancy hit it off right away. When she left he hugged her and said, "Will you come to Wendy's with us?" What can I say? Inviting a new friend to come to lunch with us is the nicest compliment Vincent can pay anyone.

If this book sounds like a love letter to Wendy's–you're right. It is. Life has changed for the better since we began going to Wendy's every week. Are all the changes in my life because we eat at Wendy's? Maybe, maybe not. But life is good and I'm not taking any chances.

If you want to turn your life around, try thankfulness. It will change your life mightily.—Gerald Good

Epilogue

The Rest of the Story

Praise the bridge that carried you over. —George Colman

In the twenty-plus years since we began going to Wendy's, Tom and I have faced our share of difficulties. But, although I've always been a worrier, now, surprisingly, I am on solid ground. I've learned to go with the flow, to keep my head, and not let the appearance of shaky ground keep me from seeing the solid truth—the only truth that matters. We have our family, our friends, our precious grandchildren, and each other. We are together, and I am grateful. Where did I learn this lesson? Amazingly, I learned it at Wendy's.

Words from an old hymn by Robert Lowry echo in my soul:

No storm can shake my inmost calm while to that rock I'm clinging. Since love is lord of heaven and earth, how can I keep from singing?

We are blessed. We have love, laughter, family, *and* we have Wendy's.

Lessons I Learned at Lunch

All great change begins at the dinner table.
—Ronald Reagan

One— Never underestimate the surprises life holds in store for you on the most ordinary days.

Two— The more grateful you are for small things, the more reasons you'll have to be grateful.

Three—Small gestures can create a lifetime of loyalty.

Four— Every one of us wants to be listened to, loved, and appreciated.

Five— Family is defined, not by the bonds of blood, but by the ties of affection.

Six— There is no substitute for showing up.

Seven—The most minor occasion can be a cause for great joy and celebration—if you let it.

Eight— You create relationships by listening, not by talking.

Nine— Respect, good manners, and love prevails over any cultural, political or religious differences.

And finally…

Ten— There's always room for one more.

As each day comes to us refreshed and anew, so does my gratitude renew itself daily. The breaking of the sun over the horizon is my grateful heart dawning upon a blessed world.—Terri Guillemets